T0306007

HOLISTIC BUSINESS PROCESS MANAGEMENT

Japanese Management and International Studies
(ISSN: 2010-4448)

Editor-in-Chief: Yasuhiro Monden *(University of Tsukuba, Japan)*

Published

Vol. 4 International Management Accounting in Japan:
Current Status of Electronics Companies
edited by Kanji Miyamoto

Vol. 5 Business Process Management of Japanese and Korean Companies
*edited by Gunyung Lee, Masanobu Kosuga, Yoshiyuki Nagasaka &
Byungkyu Sohn*

Vol. 6 M&A for Value Creation in Japan
edited by Yasuyoshi Kurokawa

Vol. 7 Business Group Management in Japan
edited by Kazuki Hamada

Vol. 8 Management of an Inter-Firm Network
edited by Yasuhiro Monden

Vol. 9 Management of Service Businesses in Japan
*edited by Yasuhiro Monden, Noriyuki Imai, Takami Matsuo &
Naoya Yamaguchi*

Vol. 10 Management of Enterprise Crises in Japan
edited by Yasuhiro Monden

Vol. 11 Entrepreneurship in Asia: Social Enterprise, Network and Grossroots
Case Studies
*edited by Stephen Dun-Hou Tsai, Ted Yu-Chung Liu, Jersan Hu &
Shang-Jen Li*

Vol. 12 Lean Management of Global Supply Chain
edited by Yasuhiro Monden & Yoshiteru Minagawa

Vol. 13 Management of Innovation Strategy in Japanese Companies
edited by Kazuki Hamada & Shufuku Hiraoka

Vol. 14 Holistic Business Process Management: Theory and Practice
edited by Gunyung Lee, Masanobu Kosuga & Yoshiyuki Nagasaka

For the complete list of titles in this series, please go to
http://www.worldscientific.com/series/jmis

Japanese Management and International Studies – Vol. 14

HOLISTIC BUSINESS PROCESS MANAGEMENT

editors

Gunyung Lee
Niigata University, Japan

Masanobu Kosuga
Kwansei Gakuin University, Japan

Yoshiyuki Nagasaka
Kwansei Gakuin University, Japan

World Scientific

EW JERSEY · LONDON · SINGAPORE · BEIJING · SHANGHAI · HONG KONG · TAIPEI · CHENNAI · TOKYO

Published by

World Scientific Publishing Co. Pte. Ltd.

5 Toh Tuck Link, Singapore 596224

USA office: 27 Warren Street, Suite 401-402, Hackensack, NJ 07601

UK office: 57 Shelton Street, Covent Garden, London WC2H 9HE

British Library Cataloguing-in-Publication Data
A catalogue record for this book is available from the British Library.

Japanese Management and International Studies — Vol. 14
HOLISTIC BUSINESS PROCESS MANAGEMENT
Theory and Practice

ISBN 978-981-3209-83-1

Desk Editor: Alisha Nguyen

Typeset by Stallion Press
Email: enquiries@stallionpress.com

Printed in Singapore

Japan Society of Organization and Accounting (JSOA)

Henry Aigbedo, Oakland University, USA
Mahmuda Akter, University of Dhaka, Bangladesh
Chao Hsiung Lee, National Chung Hsing University, Taiwan

Founder & Editor-in-Chief
Japanese Management and International Studies
Yasuhiro Monden, Tsukuba University, Japan

Auditor
Takeshi Ito, Value Co-Creation, Inc., Tokyo, Japan

Assistant Managers
Satoshi Arimoto, Niigata university, Japan
Hiromasa Hirai, Takasaki City University of Economics, Japan

Mission of JSOA and Editorial Information

For the purpose of making a contribution to the business and academic communities, the Japan Society of Organization and Accounting (JSOA), is committed to publishing *Japanese Management and International Studies* (JMIS), **which is a refereed annual publication with a specific theme for each volume.** It is on Thomson Reuters Web of Science.

Focusing on Japan and Japan-related issues, the series is designed to inform the world about research outcomes of the new "Japanese-style management system" developed in Japan. However, as the series title suggests, it also promotes *"International Studies"* on the interface of managerial competencies between Japan and other countries that include Asian countries as well as Western countries under the globalized business activities of Japanese companies.

Research topics included in this series are management of organizations in a broad sense (including the business group or inter-firm network) and the accounting for managing the organizations. More specifically, topics include business strategy, business models, organizational restoration, corporate finance, M&A, environmental management, operations management, managerial & financial accounting, manager performance evaluation, reward systems. The research approach is interdisciplinary, which includes case studies, theoretical studies, normative studies and empirical studies, but emphasizes real world business.

Our JSOA's board of directors has established an editorial board of international standing. In each volume, guest editors who are experts on the volume's special theme serve as the volume editors. The details of JSOA is shown in its by-laws contained in the home-page: http://jsoa. sakura.ne.jp/english/index.html

Editorial Board

Eri Yokota, Keio University, Japan
Péter Horváth, Horváth & Partners, Germany
Arnd Huchzermeier, WHU Koblenz, Germany
Christer Karlsson, Copenhagen Business School, Denmark
Rolf G Larsson, Lund University, Sweden
Jose Antonio Dominguez Machuca, University of Sevilla, Spain
Luis E. Carretero Diaz, Universidad Complutense, Spain
John Y. Lee, Pace University, USA
Kenneth A. Merchant, University of Southern California, USA
Jimmy Y.T. Tsay, National Taiwan University, Taiwan
Stephen DunHou Tsai, National Sun Yat-Sen University, Taiwan
Yanghon Chung, KAIST, Korea
Mohammad Aghdassi, Tarbiat Modarres University, Iran
Mahfuzul Hoque, University of Dhaka, Bangladesh
Walid Zaramdini, Al Akhawayn University, Morocco

About the Editors

 Gunyung Lee is a Professor in the Faculty of Economics at Niigata University in Japan. He has been majoring in management accounting. He received his Ph.D. from the University of Tsukuba. He is the former President of Japan Society of Organization and Accounting (JSOA). His current research interests mainly focus on the development of a cost management model in Business Process Management for small and medium-sized enterprises (SMEs). He has published many articles and books in three languages, English, Japanese, and Korean. His recent publications include "Original Management Accounting Technique of Kyocera: Harmony of Amoeba Management Philosophy and Profit Center, *Korean Journal of Accounting Research,* Vol. 20 No. 5, October 2015, pp. 287–311(in Korean)" and *"Business Process Management of Japanese and Korean Companies*, edited by Gunyung Lee, Masanobu Kosuga, Yoshiyuki Nagasaka and Byungkyu Sohn, World Scientific, 2010".

Email: lee@econ.niigata-u.ac.jp or gylee7@gmail.com

Masanobu Kosuga is a Professor of School of Business Administration, Kwansei Gakuin University, Nishinomiya, Japan. He has been majoring in cost and management accounting. He received B. A., MBA, and Ph. D. from Kwansei Gakuin University. He is a Director of Japan Accounting Association (JAA), a former Senior Director of Japanese Association of Management Accounting (JAMA), and a former President of Japan Cost Accounting Association (JCAA). His current research interests mainly focus on Strategic Management Accounting. He is the Chairman of JAA Special Committee (2015–2017) on "Strategic Management and Management Accounting". He has published many articles and books in English and Japanese. His main publications include "*Behavioral Theory of Budgeting*, 2nd edition, Chuo-keizai-sha, 1997 (in Japanese)," and "*Japanese Management Accounting Today*, co-edited by Y. Monden, *et al.*, World Scientific, 2007".

Email: masa-kos@kwansei.ac.jp

Yoshiyuki Nagasaka is a Professor in the Faculty of Business Administration, Konan University. He received his B. S., M. S. and Ph. D. degrees in Engineering from Osaka University in 1981, 1983 and 1992, respectively. In 1974, he joined Komatsu Ltd. as a researcher. From 1987 to 1989, he studied at the University of British Columbia, Canada. From 1994 to 2001, he was an Associate Professor in the Faculty of Department of Business Administration, Osaka Sangyo University. He moved to Konan University in 2001. His research interests include Business Process Management, Information Technology, and Cost Management. Now, he is Vice Chairman, Japan Society of Organization and Accounting. He has published many articles and books in English and Japanese. His recent publications include "*Business Process Management of Japanese and Korean Companies*, edited by Gunyung Lee, Masanobu Kosuga, Yoshiyuki Nagasaka and Byungkyu Sohn, World Scientific, 2010".

Email: nagaska@konan-u.ac.jp

List of Contributors

Gunyung Lee
Professor, Faculty of Economics, Niigata University, Japan

Masanobu Kosuga
Professor, School of Business Administration, Kwansei Gakuin University, Japan

Yoshiyuki Nagasaka
Professor, Faculty of Business Administration, Konan University, Japan

Aiko Kageyama
MBA, School of Business Administration,
Kwansei Gakuin University, Japan
Former Research Fellow, Hiroshima University, Japan

Yoko Asakura
Associate Professor, School of International Professional Development,
College of International Professional Development,
Kansai Gaidai University, Japan

Kenji Hirayama
President & CEO, Gimbal LLC, Japan

Kyounghwan Cha
Managing Consultant, IT Service Co. Ltd., Korea

Seungchan Lee
Managing Consultant, IT Service Co. Ltd., Korea

Suyong Kim
Senior Consultant, IT Service Co. Ltd., Korea

Hyunjong Yoo
Assistant Consultant, IT Service Co. Ltd., Korea

Hiroyuki Matsumoto
Representative Director, 956 Inc., Japan

Noriyuki Imai
Part-time Professor, Graduate School of Business,
Meijo University, Japan

Contents

Preface

Business Process Management (BPM) refers to *"the control and management of transactions between organizations both within and outside corporations by viewing the transaction flows as processes, which is enabled by breaking up the traditional walls between organizations, sharing information and resources among them, and combining and connecting their transactions"*.

In today's world, we are experiencing major environmental changes that are characterized by the development of internet and cut-throat competition between firms. Widespread availability of information and fierce competition among suppliers has resulted in bargaining power shifting from suppliers to buyers and consumers. Consequently, firms have begun to feel the need to evaluate their performance from the perspective of their customers. The approach of BPM is considered a solution for fulfilling this need. BPM is increasingly being looked at more closely today due to the innovations in the information technology (IT) space where visualization of business processes and sharing of information has become possible. However, recent research on BPM has focused largely on the visualization of business process by using IT. We believe that the research on BPM must be linked with the existing tools of management.

This book focuses on building BPM as a management model, addressing the importance of BPM views, analyzing the effectiveness of the approach, and studying the research trends in BPM. The book also describes case studies of Japanese and Korean companies and BPM models suitable for small and medium-sized enterprises (SMEs) recommending the original IT solution. To summarize, the purpose of this book is to construct and discuss a BPM model based on oriental views. This book, based on the new results of researches and case studies, is the second book that has been written after the publication of *Business Process Management of Japanese and Korean Companies* by World Scientific Ltd. in 2010.

For exploring the above purpose, we will provide the following three areas as our research themes to the readers:

PART I: **Theory and Methodology of BPM**
PART II: **Case Studies of BPM in Japanese and Korean Companies**
PART III: **Action Research of BPM in Japanese Small and Medium-Sized Enterprises**

The structure of the volume, describing how the above-mentioned intentions of the book have been addressed in each part, is as follows.

Part I. Theory and Methodology of BPM

In Part 1, priority is given to clarifying the theoretical aspects of the basic BPM structure. This part initially describes the framework of the BPM model, followed by various theoretical aspects of BPM including business process innovation under varying conditions, management information systems used in BPM, and influence of global environments.

The first paper in Part I divides BPM into two fragments — process management and process strategy. This paper provides the framework about how to understand, construct, manage, and evaluate an organization's business processes internally and externally to ensure customer satisfaction.

The second paper examines the features and the problems of time-driven activity-based costing (TD-ABC) from the perspective of practicability, and compares it with the proposed process-oriented ABC (PO-ABC) through a numerical example. This paper also shows that collaboration of BPM with PO-ABC allows for effective cost accounting and cost control.

The third paper introduces the business process re-engineering case study that utilizes the key performance indicator (KPI) pool. The case study is of a Japanese company that produces small and medium-sized liquid crystals that utilized the KPI pool in a supply chain management (SCM) project.

The fourth paper presents the application of Toyota Production System (TPS) in the current context, where the goal of a mature TPS is to shift its focus from productivity improvement within the manufacturing process to ensuring a customer-oriented and a cross-sectional BPM in order to increase adaptability to customer needs by offering diversified, high-quality products with minimal lead-time.

Part II. Case Studies on BPM in Japanese and Korean Companies

Part II consists of four papers on BPM practices in Japanese and Korean companies. The authors attempt to describe the current state of BPM practices in Japan and Korea.

The first paper sums up the main findings of the research on the cost management practices in Japanese Company A (name withheld on request). This case explores the implications of *Quality-focused Cost Management* practices by projects from the viewpoint of BPM. It illustrates the role for cost information in a Japanese construction firm.

The second paper summarizes the main findings of the research undertaken on BPM practices in *Panasonic Corporation* of Japan. It explores how and why Panasonic Corporation has been pursuing *Business Process Innovations* so actively.

The third paper discusses how *Canon Inc.* of Japan executes process management. In particular, this paper addresses how reconstruction and management of processes have been undertaken for the purpose of business expansion.

The fourth paper presents a case study that describes the management systems and the BPM introduction process in a Korean IT services company. This paper examines the background, the approaching measure of BPM, BPM project procedure detail, and achievement of BPM adaption through the project in Korean Company A.

Part III. Action Research of BPM in Japanese Small and Medium-Sized Enterprises

Part III introduces the results of the action research undertaken by the BPM study group to construct and manage BPM for SMEs.

The first paper introduces the management and the construction methodology of a business process appropriate for SMEs, as shortage of funds and talented workers typically makes it difficult for SMEs to adapt BPM.

The second paper introduces the IT tool "SCRUM" that is used for business processes measurements once BPM has been applied. We also explore the application of SCRUM in *Tamazawa Seiki Co., Ltd.* of Japan.

Acknowledgments

The editors are very grateful to Alisha Nguyen, the executive editor of Social Science in World Scientific Publishing Company for her various invaluable efforts to make this volume a reality. Ms. Philly Lim, the desk editor, is also much appreciated for handling our manuscripts. Furthermore, I would like to express special thanks to Professor Emeritus of the University of Tsukuba, Yasuhiro Monden, the founder of Japan Society Organization and Accounting (JSOA), who made it possible for us to publish this book as book series Vol. 14. Finally, the authors who worked for this volume will be amply rewarded if it contributes new ideas or knowledge to the literature on business management, information management and Asian management, thereby being of some use to people around the world.

Gunyung Lee
Principal Volume Editor
October 2017

PART I

Theory and Methodology of BPM

The Conceptual Framework of Business Process Management

Gunyung Lee

Professor, Faculty of Economics, Niigata University

1. Introduction

It is generally known that today's era — the IT era — is characterized by the global spread of information networks using Information Technology and the Internet in the IT era, corporate activities both inside and outside the corporation, are conducted in multiple areas simultaneously and surpass the hitherto existing limits of time and space. Because of this historical background and the complete environmental change to cutthroat competition, the leadership in commercial deals has shifted from suppliers to buyers. Consequently, the suppliers' appropriate response to buyers' and customers' demands becomes one of the primary means to achieve a competitive advantage. Hence, in order to respond to the power wielded by customers (buyers and end-users), the suppliers need to customize their products and services according to the customers' tastes and desires to cater to the likes of each customer.

It is necessary to (1) move the managerial point from the conventional vertical communication system usually found in organizations to a horizontal communication system and (2) establish a Business Process Management (BPM) system that can speedily and flexibly manage its responses to such environmental changes. This paper will discuss a framework that incorporates the understanding, construction, management, and evaluation of the business process both inside and outside the corporation such that the customers are satisfied in the competitive environment in the IT era.

2. Necessity and Possibility of Process Management in the IT Era

We live in a fast-paced world where things are constantly changing; therefore, it is increasingly difficult to predict what will happen in the near future. Moreover, the development of information that allows one to circumnavigate the limits of time and space on global business transactions has been altering the corporate environment in various ways. This environmental change necessitates that companies swiftly match the input of environmental changes with corporate output. In particular, because of the traditional response which focuses on functions often results in an accumulation of information and materials due to the imbalance among functions and the barriers among the many functions, there is a need for a swift response to the environmental changes from the process management perspective. In the IT era, the necessity of and possibilities for process management are being propounded simultaneously by the following two demands (Monden *et al.*, 2007, pp. 235–248).

2.1. *Demand from the management side*

The leadership in commercial deals has shifted from vendors to customers due to the easy access to the Internet and cutthroat competition, and hence, a company needs to plan and offer its products or services in line with the customers' views. In other words, there is a need for horizontal organization management that considers the customer as the starting point.

Meanwhile, triggered by the window dressing settlement of Enron and WorldCom, the Corporate Reform Act (Sarbanes–Oxley Act: the SOX act) was executed for its recurrence prevention in the US. This act imposes a duty of the construction and accountability of internal control to which a manager guarantees the reliability of financial statements. In this act, the same duty is also imposed on both the US and the non-US companies. This strengthening of the supervisor function of managers or inspectorial agencies to such internal control requires a business process to be managed and documented appropriately. The aim of this law was to improve the reliability of financial statements by clarifying a business process; however, it is understood that, at the same time, a business process must be built to guarantee competitive advantage. Therefore, following changes in a company's environment, such as a surge of customer power, there is an increase in expectation from process management as well as in legal demands for the preparation and application of internal control.

These demands from the management side can be attained by a system that integrates material flow and information flow. Therefore, the construction of a BPM system that can manage the performance of the business process based on the customer's view is deemed most valuable as an important means to cater to the demands from the management side.

2.2 Support from innovation in IT

In the 1990s, Business Process Reengineering (BPR) approaches that tried to achieve a drastic restructuring of the business process using IT failed because they were unable to obtain the expected support from IT. In the latter half of the 1990s, information management using Enterprise Resource Planning (ERP) originated as a result of the failure of these BPR approaches. However, ERP confined the operations into a concrete box, which was unable to support the changing operation flow. Hence, in the 2000s, (1) Service Oriented Architecture (SOA) technology that has enabled the restructuring of the IT environment to allow it to respond more flexibly to the environmental changes and (2) various softwares (Harmon, 2010, pp. 75–77) that have enabled the support of the changing operation flow flexibly have been developed. These are effective tools for the construction of BPM system because these new abilities can be exercised to create the business process and assess real-time performance management virtually.

3. History of BPM

In today's IT era, information is treated on a global scale, the power of information spreads around all areas, and information control has become a means of producing competitive advantage. Moreover, in the global competitive environment, past experiences of success lose their worthiness, and management must always monitor changes in the environment, respond speedily, and obtain the outcome with certainty. However, organizational goals and management resources are distributed using a top-down approach based on the vertical organization. As a result, a mismatch frequently arises in the supply and consumption of resources due to the partition between the function and the department. This becomes an obstacle to achieving the expected goal. Therefore, establishment of a new management technique from the resource-consumption point of view is required.

However, according to the results of the Internet questionnaire targeting the readers of a Web magazine (*Business Process Trends*) in 2006 for the purpose of investigating the company trend, BPM was not recognized as a broadly accepted fixed model, as shown in Fig. 1; in other words, BPM has not managed to become more than just a way to share information within the organization by IT and to support decision making. Nevertheless, some companies have been able to manage the process using BPM to a considerable extent. Moreover, through IT innovation, it is becoming possible to build and manage BPM at low cost.

As long as the term "BPM" refers to the management of the business process of horizontal organization, we can say that the origin of process management dates back to the Tailorist approaches. On the other hand, it is said that the trigger that led to the recognition of BPM in Europe and the US was the Total Quality Management (TQM) approach adopted in the 1980s (Jeston & Nelis, 2006, pp. xii–xvi). In the 1990s, European and American companies faced a stagnant market and cutthroat competition across the globe. This led to further development of the ideas of traditional

Which of the following best describes-what BPM means to you?	Number	Ratio (%)
1. An approach to process redesign or improvement	61	18
2. A cost-saving initiative focused on increasing productivity	21	6
3. A set of software technologies for automating and managing runtime business processes	79	23
4. A management philosophy that focuses on organizing the business around its business processes	**187**	**54**
Total	348	100

Fig. 1.   Survey results on the meaning of BPM submitted by the management over the world
Source: Celia & Harmon (2007).

process management, and new methods such as BPR and Six Sigma emerged. BPR was suggested by Hammar in 1990. His article "Don't automate, obliterate" in the *Harvard Business Review* (1990) was the starting point from which BPR disseminated quickly. Although BPR aimed to drastically restructure the business process using IT, IT was unable to describe and support the complicated processes (Jeston & Nelis, 2006, pp. xii–xvi).

Drawing upon the lessons learned from the failure of BPR, ERP was introduced in the latter half of the 1990s. It appeared as though ERP had already solved the process management problem related to IT; however, ERP was unable to support process improvement because it suffered from many shortcomings including non-flexibility, despite the fact that it was sold with the catchphrase *"best practice"*. In other words, after ERP was set up, the flexibility of the process was lost and could be likened to dry concrete, even though initially (before installation), ERP was as flexible as wet cement (Smith & Finger, 2007, p. 73).

There are two opinions regarding the origin of BPM. One is that it originated in the 1990s (Jeston & Nelis 2006, pp. xii–xvi) and the other is that it emerged after the year 2000 (Jeston & Nelis, 2006; Smith & Finger, 2007). However, it seems that the difference between these two opinions arises from (1) the time frame of the emergence of IT that supports process management and (2) the history of process management. The latter viewpoint emphasizes IT innovation that supplements the lack of flexibility in ERP. This viewpoint treats BPM according to the development of the Business Process Management System (BPMS), i.e., as a total management system of business process that supports a flexible unity between business process and IT. However, a consensus regarding the content of BPM is yet to be reached and BPM has been reduced to a three-letter acronym used to refer to process management.

Harmon (2010, pp. 37–38) showed that there are three streams in the methodology for the management of a business process. These are streams of management, Quality Control (QC) and IT. Each stream has mutually ignored the other streams or degraded their worthiness until now. However, Harmon stated that the three streams have now been included in comprehensive BPM.

4. The Concept of Process

A process is a series of interlinked activities that achieve a specific objective (Daly & Freeman, 1997, p. 16). Davenport (1993, p. 5), however, defines the process as follows: "A process is simply a structured, measurable set of activities designed to produce a specified output for a particular customer or market". Therefore, we can say that the definition of process differs with each person. This is the reason why each writer defines the process differently on the basis of the measurement unit, categorization, and extent of the process.

This paper regards the process as "a flow composed of various mutually dependent groups of activities toward the creation of customer value, the input and the output of which are clearly distinguished, and which have a hierarchical structure depending on the levels of the subject matters of management". In addition, it is desirable for the process to satisfy the following three key elements as explained in Statements on Management Accounting (SMA) No.4NN (2000, p. 8).

Transformation: By means of one or more changes, it provides output from a group of interrelated work activities that is of greater value than the inputs.

Feedback control: Involves some regulatory means by which the transformation activities are modified or collected to maintain certain attributes of the output.

Repeatability: Implies that a process is executed many times in the same manner.

5. Process Classification Framework (PCF) of the American Productivity & Quality Center (APQC)

Supply-chain operations reference (SCOR) of the Supply Chain Council (SCC) is a well-known business process framework. SCOR is composed of three levels. SCC formulates the process framework until level 3, and the individual firm builds level 4 based on the condition of its company. In addition to SCOR, other frameworks include the Value Reference Model (VRM) built by the Value Chain Group, eTOM developed for a telecom company, and the APQC framework that incorporates the base elements of SCOR (Harmon, 2010, pp. 61–63).

In particular, the free benchmarking service SCORmark, which is provided for SCC members and operated by SCC, APQC, and IBM together, is an available reference model for BPM construction. However, Harmon (2010, pp. 72–74) pointed out that as some companies are building various simple to very complex processes, the above-mentioned standardized processes can only be used as reference models. In addition, because the management of complex processes is difficult, companies are required to clarify the management purpose of the processes.

6. Process Management Unit and Operation Flow

In process management, the process initiated by the event will be described as a management unit on the basis of the partitions of the connected function and activity. In other words, it is necessary to solve the issue of how to describe and define the process as a management unit. The process management unit is an inter-departmental specific process wherein the output is repeatedly delivered from the flow of activities connected to two or more departments. The *event* is the occurrence that starts the process. Therefore, the event differs from the function that uses time. Further, as shown in Fig. 2, the event is related to a point in time. The process controls the functions in the sense that it is the process that uses a function or the connected functions as a set of activities (Seidelmeier, 2004, pp. 70–71).

Davenport (1993, p. 28) explains the basis for the decision about the length of the process as follows:

The objective of process identification is the key to making these definitions and determining their implications. If the objective is incremental improvement, it is sufficient to work with many narrowly defined processes, as the risk of failure is relatively low. But when the objective is radical process change, a process must be defined as broadly as possible.

Davenport (1993, p. 31) also adds that process definition is more of an art than science.

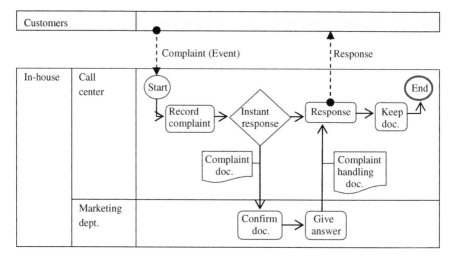

Fig. 2.   Example of a trouble-shooting process
Source: Takeyasu *et al.* (2007, p. 3); modified by author.

Meanwhile, the Software Engineering Institute (SEI) of the Carnegie Mellon University developed the Capability Maturity Model Integrated (CMMI) in 1987 to systematically evaluate the construction and control level of a process, as shown in the Fig. 3. CMMI is a criterion of judgment that diverts the developed method in order to evaluate the development level of the software and identifies the standardized process level that matches with the actual operation level. That is, even if the company has a business process model, the control levels of a process will differ depending on which level the process construction is progressing.

On the other hand, it is relatively easy to construct a barometer that estimates whether a specific process is working efficiently. However, it is difficult to estimate whether the given process contributes to the outcome of a company. Therefore, a method that systemically connects a business goal and a process target is necessary, and a Balanced Scorecard (BSC) can be used in this matter. However, a traditional BSC focuses on the performance measure of a function or department rather than the process itself. In the field of process valuation research, application of a BSC that links a department performance measure and a process performance

Fig. 3.   The CMM model with five levels of maturity

Source: http://www.bptrends.com/publicationfiles/spotlight_051909.pdf.

measure is gaining attention recently (Harmon, 2010, pp. 66–67). In the conventional result-oriented approach, operating performance is measured and evaluated using the following steps (Castellano *et al.*, 2004):

(1) Assign a performance target to the applicant (department).
(2) Combine the realization value of a target and a key performance indicator.
(3) Measure the realized value against the target for every fixed period.
(4) Reward.

However, this approach possesses the following disadvantages:

(1) Generally, a targeted value is fixed arbitrarily.
(2) A targeted value does not consider the actual result or capacity of the present process.
(3) It does not consider the correlation within the processes in a goal-setting process.
(4) It does not understand the connection between the realized performance value and performing-a-task method.

Moreover, Kittredge (2004) stated that one main reason why the roles of management accounting and process management differ is that the viewpoint of a measurement barometer is not in harmony. In a BSC, the strategic goal is deployed up to the performance-evaluating indicators of operations. However, the perceptions of the manager or the process manager concerning the performance measurements are different when the measurement criterion of the operations is not linked with the strategy or when the criterion is not integrated through the management units of the function and the process, and so forth. As a result, it is easy to execute a strategy that is not accepted by the workers in the field. Kittredge (2004) insists that such problems can be solved if the performance indicators conform to the measurement indicators of the strategically and tactically important processes chosen by the process managers are reflected in the BSC and these indicators are deployed on the BSC.

7. Structure of BPM

BPM is "the control and management of transactions between organizations both inside and outside corporations by viewing the transaction flows as processes, which is enabled by breaking up the traditional walls between organizations, sharing information and resources among them, and combining and connecting their transactions" (Lee *et al.* 2009). To sum up, BPM has the following features:

(1) Evaluate the *process as a management unit.*
(2) Focus on the *consumption of resources of a horizontal organization* instead of on the supply of resources of a vertical organization.
(3) *Visualize* a process with IT support.
(4) Perform *visualized control* by sharing process information within the organization.
(5) Promote *performance improvement* by using process information from the perspective of *cost/time/capacity.*

This paper divides BPM into two: a *process chain management* inside the corporation that surpasses the functional and departmental barriers and a *process net strategy* outside the corporation that surpasses the barriers among corporations.

7.1. *Process chain management*

In an organization that focuses on functions, the business operation is managed because of the function, and managers naturally consume and manage resources according to the functional budget and emphasize the strict adaptation of standards. Consequently, because employees are eager to observe the functional standards and save resources, the relationships among business process, suppliers, and customers are not optimized (Department of Defense, 1994). Gradually, there emerges an expectation that process chain management will remove the barriers among the functions as shown in Fig. 4 to optimize the whole value chain by completing link A and integrate the main process with the support process by completing link B. IT innovation enhances the possibility of this action. On the other hand, it is said that in today's competitive environment, a large company does not defeat a smaller one, but a fast company defeats a slower one.

However, under the uncertain environment that cannot correspond at a speed alone, there is a demand for a process management system that can manage the process promptly and flexibly according to the changes in the market environment. For such a process management system, it is necessary to achieve a balance between the *value chain* (to manage the process in a horizontal organization) and *management chain* (to manage the horizontal organization using the Plan–Do–Check–Action (PDCA) cycle).

In other words, the process PDCA cycle rather than the departmental PDCA cycle that occurs within the department is preferable for the systematic, integrated, continuous improvement of the whole process; this is

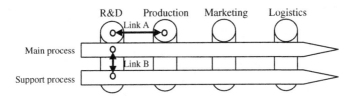

Fig. 4.   Value-chain optimization of business process

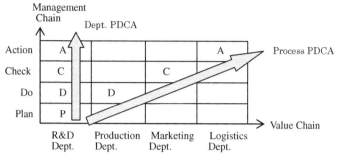

Fig. 5.   Value chain and process PDCA

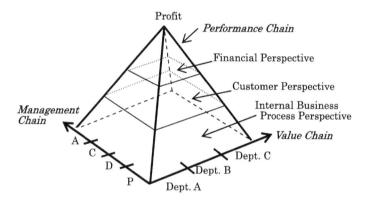

Fig. 6.   Integration of the three chains

shown in Fig. 5. That is, the management system is expected to perform the process PDCA cycle for all the processes across all departments. As a result, process management aims for optimal harmony between the *value chain* of business processes and the *management chain*, which allows us to overcome the traditional walls between organizations and carry out the management cycle of the organization's management. However, in order to connect the outcome of process management to financial performance through a *performance chain*, the operating performance of a process must be measured (see Fig. 6).

In BSC, the lead indicators are the performance drivers and lag indicators are the outcomes. The *lag indicator* only identifies the present position and illustrates the change in the indicator. However, the *lead indicator* identifies the destination and requires an early decision. Therefore, we can say that the lead indicator is preferable in process management when it comes to the real-time management of the performance.

In general, the effect of the change in the process on the consumption of resources in the process can be easily identified; however, estimating the reverse is not that easy. If performance management and process management harmonize in the manner mentioned above, the process can be managed by using the performance chain as shown in Fig. 6. In other words, important performance drivers that yield the desired outcome in BSC can be systemically linked with the strategic goal if they are chosen from each of the process outputs. In addition, in BSC, we can also determine the direction of the process management. As a result, at the process level, the targets determined using a top-down approach match the management indicators chosen using the bottom-up approach, and the application of PDCA cycle on BSC becomes possible, such that an integrated management system, as depicted in Fig. 6, can be constructed.

7.2. Process net strategy

The competitive environment has already shifted from competition among companies to competition among process networks that aim to construct a syndicate. In such an environment, the selection, concentration, and collaboration strategies of the process, such as inter-firm process-level alliances, shared services, and outsourcing part of the business process, are adopted because of the expectation that these steps will yield competitive advantage. It is said that the strategic process net construction can be divided into the four following strategies (Yamada & Uchida, 1999):

(1) Choose and manage only the function that becomes the key of the competitive advantage within the existing value chain and outsource with the rest to realize lower costs.
(2) Aim toward creating an oligopoly in particular processes by focusing on special processes within the existing value chain that add significant value and supplying the same to multiple companies.

(3) Streamline the value chain by cutting the unnecessary processes and focus on customer satisfaction.

(4) Add value by adding new functions when the customers' needs exceed the capability of the existing value chain.

In other words, the process net strategy is a decision-making approach whereby the processes are selected and concentrated on the basis of the corporate strategy as well as considering the plausible changes in the environment. This approach is adopted both inside and outside the company/country.

Using a strategy that secures the functional advantage in the value chain under a competitive environment, the company is confronted with a decision-making problem — of whether to buy the functional advantage or develop it. In general, in an industry where environmental changes are not that intense, it is preferable for the company to choose the strategy of developing the functional advantage so as to always sustain the mainspring of long-term growth. However, when long-term growth is somewhat elusive, this strategy has a negative effect in that it increases costs. Consequently, the strategy of buying the functional advantage needs to be constructed by the *collaboration of the business process* such as the selection, the concentration, and the collaboration of the business process.

7.2.1. *Business process collaboration*

In today's competitive environment, which is characterized by increasing uncertainty and severity, it is necessary to decrease the risk generated by environmental changes and adopt strategic means to maintain and expand one's competitive advantage. In other words, it is necessary to invest limited managerial resources to identify and foster a process that may become a core competence and to utilize resources outside the corporation, if necessary, for processes other than core competence. This approach is deemed feasible because using other corporations' assets, rather than creating or buying new assets necessary to respond to environmental changes, can decrease the economic risk and also because this improves corporate flexibility and enables the company to respond to environmental changes in a short amount of time (Hagel, 2003).

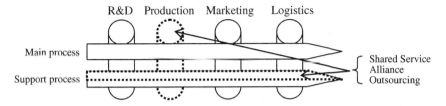

Fig. 7.   Business process collaboration

However, this approach does necessitate that an intra-corporate process network that smoothly connects processes across multiple corporations and that exchanges real-time information regarding the same is built. As this problem is, to a great extent, solvable using the Internet, and in particular, the Web services architecture, such as business process networks are possible. Therefore, in the information era, it is said that the company that shares information attains more success than the company that manages information. Fig. 7 depicts a case wherein the product is procured from an Electronics Manufacturing Services (EMS) company, i.e., outsourcing, and the data processing is delegated to a special company, i.e., shared service.

7.2.2. Patterns of business process collaboration

In this paper, alliance, outsourcing, and shared service, etc. are considered as the main examples of business process collaboration. However, it is not easy to define business process collaboration because the above-mentioned features and their ranges can be changed. Therefore, the paper proposes that the collaboration is considered to have taken place when the company performs the following activities in the business process network across companies.

Outsourcing: Some particular processes except the processes that the company performs are delegated to another company (or other companies).

Shared service: Similar processes that the companies perform are concentrated together.

Alliance: Some processes that the company performs are supplemented by the cooperating company.

In the IT industry, the system of cheaply procuring components from third parties and assembling them in-house is being generalized. The company with the horizontal-division-of-labor type business structure is the case. However, there also exist companies that have adopted a reverse strategy and have extended their profits. There are cases of companies with the vertical-division-of-labor type business structures. If we selected the case of liquid crystal TV, Sony of Japan has a horizontal-division-of-labor type and Samsung of South Korea has a vertical-division-of-labor type structure. If panels of liquid crystal TVs can be procured from outside companies at low price, there will be no need for insourcing the panel through vertical integration. The vertical integration type, which involves intentional investment and in-house production, becomes less beneficial, and the horizontal-division-of-labor model becomes dominant instead. However, Samsung produces the panel in-house with a vertical integration type and is still gaining profits. This is because they have an absolute sales amount that can cover both fixed and variable costs (Nikkei Business, 2011). Depending on how the company responds to the current circumstances, it will use the vertical-division-of-labor type strategy of taking an investment risk or the horizontal-division-of-labor type strategy of responding to the risk of demand fluctuation.

8. Conclusion

While many new process management techniques have been proposed recently, BPM is the general term used to refer to these. However, process-oriented management is not a new concept in business management; in fact, process-oriented management was simply not feasible until now. Today, cooperation and integration among business processes, which hitherto were impossible, have become possible because data processing and telecommunication have evolved a great deal due to advancements in IT. On the other hand, process management is also required to effectively respond to the changes in the highly competitive environment not only with respect to customer satisfaction but also with time, flexibility, and cost.

Though many companies have attempted process restructuring (e.g., BPR), few have achieved their objectives. It seems that this might be the case because these companies did not establish a process management mechanism to improve the efficiency of the entire process and ensure the stability of the reformed processes, which are the problems of BPR that were mentioned in this paper. Hence, while many new process management techniques to overcome such problems are being proposed today, it is not easy to create a systematical method of process management to improve the efficiency and stability of the restructured process. In the current environment, where the changes are intense and unforeseeable and any past success or experience has lost its meaning, BPM, which allows the synchronization of the company's output with the changes in the environment, will be an effectual tool to obtain competitive advantage.

References

Castellano, J. F., Young, S., Anderson, D. & McLean, W. (2004). Process-based Measurements: The Key to more Effective Decision Making, *Cost Management*, pp. 5–14.

Celia, W. & Harmon, P. (2007). Business Process Management and Service Oriented Architecture. http://www.bptrends.com/bptrends-surveys/.

Daly, C. & Freeman, T. (1997). *The Road of to Excellence: Becoming a Process-Based Company* (*The CAM-I Process Management Guide*), Institute of Management Accountants, CAM-I.

Davenport, T. H. (1993). *Process Innovation — Reengineering Work Through Information Technology*, Harvard Business School Press.

Department of Defense. (1994). www.c3i.osd.mil/bpr/bprcd/mhome.htm.

Hagel, III. J. (2002). Leveraged Growth: Expanding Sales Without Sacrificing Profits, *Diamond Harvard Business Review*, pp. 68–77.

Hammer, M. & Champy, J. (1990). Reengineering Work: Don't Automate, Obliterate, *Harvard Business Review*, pp. 104–112.

Harmon, P. (2010). The Scope and Evolution of Business Process Management, *Handbook on Business Process Management I*, J. V. Brocke and M. Rosemann (eds.), Springer.

Jeston, J. & Nelis, J. (2006). *Business Process Management — Practical Guidelines to Successful Implementations*, Elsevier.

Kittredge, J. (2004). Process Management and Cost Management: Collaboration or Opposition, *Cost Management*, pp. 23–30.

Lee, G., Kosuga, M. & Nagasaka, Y. (2009). The Usefulness of Business Process Management in Cost Management, *The Journal of Cost Accounting Research*, Japan Cost Accounting Association, Vol. 33, No. 1, pp. 18–27 (in Japanese).

Monden, Y., Kosuga, M., Nagasaka, Y., Hiraoka, S. & Hoshi, N. (2007). *Japanese Management Accounting Today*, World Scientific.

Nikkei Business (January 31, 2011). Television War not to be Tomorrow — Samsung, the Facts of Turn to Red Figures, pp. 21–34, (in Japanese).

Seidelmeier, H. (2004). *Business Process Modeling by ARIS*, BNN (in Japanese).

Smith, H. & Finger, P. (2007). *Business Process Management: The Third Wave*, Meghan-Kiffer Press.

Statements on Management Accounting No.4NN. (2000). *Implementing Process Management for Improving Products and Services*, Institute of Management Accountants.

Takeyasu, K., Miyazaki, Y. & Higuchi, Y. (2007). *The Recording Method of Work Flow for Internal Control*, Chuokeizaisya (in Japanese).

Yamada, H. & Uchida, K. (May 10, 1999). Creative Destruction of Value Chain, *Nihon Keizai Shinbun* (in Japanese).

Process Oriented Activity-Based Costing for Business Process Management

Yoshiyuki Nagasaka
Professor, Konan University, Japan

Gunyung Lee
Professor, Niigata University, Japan

1. Introduction

A potential solution to the failure of conventional cost accounting systems to support environmental changes was proposed in the book *Relevance Lost* by Johnson & Kaplan (1987), called activity standard cost accounting (Activity-Based Costing, ABC). Nearly 30 years have passed since.

Many admit that ABC is high in rationality in theory rather than a conventional method. However, there are issues with feasibility such as the complexity of data collection or trouble with architecture, and ABC does not advance much after it is introduced to a company. The actual status of ABC/ABM of each country is as follows. Availability of ABC in the UK was 21.0% in 1994, but decreased to 17.5% in 1999, according to Innes *et al.* (2000). Ness & Cucuzza (1995) reported that less than 10% of companies in the US use ABC continuously. Around 100 companies replied to a questionnaire survey, and only 9 companies introduced ABC and 19 use ABC. Thus, only 20% of companies use ABC continuously.

Askarany & Yazdifar (2007) analyzed the correlation of the introduction and the background factor behind the introduction in this new management accounting method in Australian companies. Why is the proportion of companies introducing ABC low among Australian companies? It is due to the lack of confidence that ABC is superior to traditional cost accounting techniques in terms of complexity, compatibility, potential to see results and feasibility.

According to a study by the Institute for Nippon University Department of Commercial Science Accounts (2004), the ratio of ABC use was 23.73% in the service/non-manufacturing industry and 8.99% in the manufacturing industry in Japan. Japanese companies must analyze the difference between the manufacturing and non-manufacturing industries. However, the low use of ABC can be summarized as issues of usefulness and feasibility. In terms of issues about usefulness, because companies determine the price of a product based on competitive markets rather than its cost and Japan has many oligopolistic markets, there is little need to collect cost information via ABC. In addition, because Japanese firms reduce costs through improvement activities on the manufacturing floor with techniques such as JIT and TQM without cost information, analytic ABC is not as necessary (Tanaka, 1993).

In the manufacturing industry, many companies do not use ABC for several reasons: (1) complicated calculations, (2) the technique is more concerned with cost management than with precise cost calculation, (3) it introduces a large expense, and (4) difficult data totalization (survey by Nippon University, Department of Commercial Science, Accounting Research Institute, 2004).

Kaplan & Anderson (2004) proposed Time-Driven Activity-Based Costing (TD-ABC) using time as the main driver to reduce the use of the driver in two phases rather than the single phase to solve the problems in conventional ABC. The authors claim that it is difficult to determine and measure the activity time conventionally, but it is easier in today's IT environment. Therefore, they state that TD-ABC has feasibility. TD-ABC is a new model that uses a time equation to measure the capacity cost ratio to calculate the time unit cost of each section and the time required for business processes, unlike conventional ABC.

Assuming that a company knows the process that represents the chain of activity, TD-ABC is a system of cost accounting for a specific process by multiplying the cost per unit time at the section and activity time in the process, collected via interviews. However, TD-ABC has problems that remain to be settled, such as the estimation of process time and the construction of the processes.

This paper first summarizes the characteristics of TD-ABC. It then examines several problems, such as handling the process in the chain of activity. The paper next proposes Process-Oriented Activity-Based Costing (PO-ABC), which can be called a development type of TD-ABC. Furthermore, the study shows that it is possible to create an effective cost accounting and cost control system with a combination of Business Process Management (BPM) and PO-ABC. The effect of BPM and PO-ABC is also discussed. BPM is the basic administrative structure of PO-ABC. The proposed model will be easily acceptable in practical business as a trial that will solve the feasibility and usefulness issues at the same time.

2. Characteristics of TD-ABC, Problems, and Improvements

2.1. Characteristics of TD-ABC

According to Kaplan & Anderson (2007a, p. 74), TD-ABC is carried out by the following procedure. Because most companies today have Enterprise Resource Planning (ERP) and Customer Relationship Management (CRM) systems, it is not difficult to collect the data required for TD-ABC. In other words, it is assumed that companies can implement TD-ABC with IT support.

(1) Financial data of the general ledger belong to each section.
(2) Section cost belong to one or more processes in the section.
(3) Load transaction data.
(4) Estimate the time required for each process and apply the time equation.
(5) Process cost belong to a cost accounting object by the time equation form.
(6) Calculation of cost and profit depending on order, [stock keeping unit (SKU), a unit of inventory management], vendor, and client.

TD-ABC has the following characteristics. In conventional ABC, the miscellaneous expenses according to the expense item of the nominal ledger is connected with an activity by a resource driver, and the activity cost is connected with an object of the cost accounting by an activity driver. However, TD-ABC contains a method to understand resource cost by section. According to Kaplan & Anderson (2007a, p. 18), the reason to use such a method is because companies understand cost according to each section, though this takes a lot of effort and many errors occur when resources cost is connected to each activity. Departmental ABC using conventional ABC was introduced by Kim *et al.* (1996) and Keys & Lefevre (1995). In their studies, they sum costs by department because there would be too much data to analyze and it is difficult to connect each data point with an activity.

The capacity cost rate in TD-ABC is calculated by dividing all departmental expenses and available total time for the on-site charge employee. The calculation does not include supervisors' or managers' time (Kaplan & Anderson, 2007b). In other words, the complicated allocation process in conventional ABC can be simplified by using time unit cost (Kaplan & Anderson, 2007a, pp. 17–18).

In TD-ABC, department costs belong to a process from the point of view of the process, which is the chain of the activity, not the bulk material of the activity, unlike in conventional ABC. An approach in TD-ABC that considers a cost count unit as a process solves the following problem (Lawson, 1994).

Because ABC System does not pay more attention to the mutual relationships of the activity and handles an activity as a solitary unit, the information about the activity obtained from conventional ABC has limitations. In other words, conventional ABC is different from the approach in the improvement according to an analysis of the mutual relationships from the strategic point of view of the whole process.

TD-ABC uses a time equation to calculate process used time. Because the process is a chain of activities, it is possible to calculate the process lead time for the total of each activity time. Then, a time equation is used to calculate activity time. Kaplan & Anderson (2007a, p. 28) describe the validity of the time equation as follows. Because they will describe the activity as required in the conventional ABC model, they use an estimator for the data, preservation quantity, throughput increase, according to the number of the variations of the activity geometrically. In TD-ABC, an additive linear equation that considers the additional time for each possible variation in the necessary basic time is constructed.

2.2. Problems with and improvement from TD-ABC

As mentioned above, it is possible to calculate the departmental expenses by following the processes of the chain of activities in TD-ABC. Process cost is calculated by multiple unit cost per hour and process lead time because the process is treated as data. Furthermore, it is a simple model in which it is possible to calculate a target cost by applying the process cost for a particular order or client. However, understanding the process concept is important to apply TD-ABC. Given enough understanding and use of the concept of the process, because a process is treated as data, it may be possible to develop TD-ABC further. This study aims to improve the feasibility and analytical ability of TD-ABC by investigating the process concept. Furthermore, this paper discusses a solution while considering several problems with TD-ABC.

2.3. Problem with and improvement of process construction in TD-ABC

In conventional ABC, the cost of the entire activity (cost pool) is related to the cost accounting object. In contrast, the calculated process cost of the chain of activities is related to the cost accounting object in TD-ABC, which is one of its characteristics. Kaplan & Anderson (2007a) describe why the process as the chain of the activity is the basis of TD-ABC as follows:

(1) Many companies have an available business processes model as its starting point (p. 35).
(2) In TD-ABC, the list of activities (Process Classification Framework, PCF) is not necessary. The linear equation for time is sufficient if the activity is diverse enough (p. 28).
(3) The scale of the model increases for a geometric series depending on the real-world complexity in ABC, but increases linearly in TD-ABC (p. 29).

Because the company must accomplish business based on task flow, business processes are built mainly in terms of the department directly responsible for the process, and the information flow is generally connected to the flow of the material. Some insist that ABC is effective in managing activities in the service industry and indirect departments. However, a company must manage many problems in order to build and manage all of its processes.

Process construction and management is difficult because the significance of the process construction is lost when it not accompanied by a structure to manage the need to change processes or address the financial results of the process according to changes in the environment. In other words, creating the process management structure to manage a process earlier increases the utility value of TD-ABC and enables an application of TD-ABC that supports a process change.

2.4. Systematization of business processes and IT tools

Because companies' business processes are connected by a complicated network, it is necessary to systematize and manage processes effectively. In BPM, giving a definite definition to a business process clarifies the obscurity of a task procedure, allowing companies to manage it efficiently. IT tools linking each application to a process described in notations such as Business Process Modeling Notation (BMMN) using computers have become popular. The American Productivity and Quality Center (APQC) and Supply Chain Council (SCC) provide a systematized standard process template that has an PCF and a Supply-Chain Operations Reference (SCOR)-model available online for practical use. There is also a free benchmarking service offered to SCC members, which provides an effective reference model for BPM construction. Called SCOR mark, it is operated jointly by the SCC, APQC, and IBM.

2.5. Problems with and potential improvements to process knowledge in TD-ABC

According to Kaplan & Anderson (2007a, pp. 27–28), the list of activities in conventional ABC has a detailed hierarchical structure to the sub-process level. On the other hand, the list of activities is not necessary in TD-ABC.

The analyst should simply estimate the capacity for the demand for resources for the variations in each activity.

However, we consider that it is necessary for a process to have a hierarchical structure and an activity. Due to the hierarchy, the company's tasks can be constructed and analyzed in detail, focusing on processes from the higher stratum to the lower stratum while confirming the characteristics of the task (fixed and non-fixed tasks, repetitive and non-repetitive duties). In addition, it is possible to compare the processes at the lower stratum to those at the higher stratum. Unlike Kaplan and Anderson's method, the model proposed in this study measures the stay time between the process and activities, and companies can manage costs using TD-ABC. Furthermore, the time equation is not necessary if the process itself is built using an IT system because this system measures the process used time automatically.

2.6. Problems with and method to improve the estimated process used time in TD-ABC

Kaplan & Anderson (2007a) describe the usefulness of the time equation and the measurement of process time and insist on superiority of TD-ABC compared to conventional ABC as follows:

(1) Based on interviews of a section employee and a manager, the business processes time is estimated and a time equation is constructed. Understanding the process time required is easy in TD-ABC, which aims to collect the right values with estimates rather than clear errors (pp. 26–27).
(2) The conventional ABC model has a high cost to determine the basic cost to assign resource costs to each activity before applying a lead time driver. Resource costs are directly allocated to cost objects by using time driver in TD-ABC, which addresses the troublesome first stage of assigning resource costs to activities and helps eliminate many potential errors (pp. 17–18).

According to Kaplan & Anderson (2007a, p. 27), a company can determine the process lead time of a task by interviewing the manager responsible for this task. However, in their method, it is not possible to know the stay time between activities or between the processes, so this is included in unused capacity. This may lead to an overestimation of the unused capacity. Furthermore, there is no method to reflect stay time in the time equation. In other words, it is hard to use this method for task improvement.

In a practical model of the management purpose of TD-ABC by Moinuddin *et al.* (2007), the value added of each activity and the non-value added are analyzed. However, it does not incorporate a solution for stay time because it does not construct the system of the process.

This entire book discusses process management. In the following, we discuss how process lead time can be measured easily using the proposed method to create and manage processes.

3. Implementation of PO-ABC by BPM

Process management in an organization requires flexibility and speed to adapt to environmental changes. Castellano *et al.* (2004) described an advantage of this approach based on a process as follows.

(1) From the process point of view, a task is carried out along a well-designed process. In addition, it is necessary to satisfy a client request by introducing the integration of the process, which is a component of the organization's system.
(2) The administrators must design, apply, supervise, and improve the processes to maintain the organization's ability to meet client requests flexibly.
(3) Meeting these goals requires a performance evaluation system based on the process view. Then, (i) the administrator obtains the information about the behavior of an important process and the existing financial results, (ii) the administrator maintains the methodology to improve the processes continuously, and (iii) this enables effective decision making.
(4) The process basis approach relies on the recognition that the results come partially from the person, and partly by the interaction of all inputs (a person, a method, materials, equipment, and environment) in the process.

This study mentioned a trial to apply TD-ABC to construct the BPM and to implement cost accounting for an organization's processes to manage financial results.

4. Cost Accounting According to Order by PO-ABC

The PO-ABC system proposed in this study is illustrated using a numerical example similar to that of Kaplan & Anderson (2004).

Fig. 1 illustrates the assumed task flow for every order. The A-order processes go only through the business department because it is an order for the company's standardized product and the B-order processes go through the business department and the production control department because the order must be customized according to the client's specifications. This example assumes that the whole activity chain for the sales department and the production control department is a mega process, and the individual activity of each section is a core process.

Furthermore, the process costs are calculated based on the department costs for 1 month and the human resources cost of the sales department and the production control department as follows:

(1) Organization system:

  (a) The sales department: 1 manager, 10 operating employees, 2 section employees.
  (b) Production control department: 1 manager, 2 section employees.

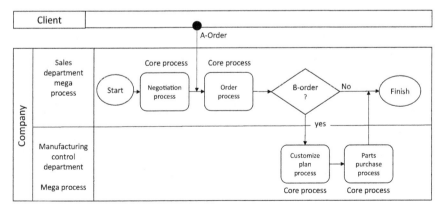

Fig. 1. Order task flows

(2) Estimation of department costs
    (a) Sales department: Direct cost and overhead cost = 748,800 dollars
    (b) Production control department: Direct cost and overhead cost = 96,000 dollars
(3) Estimation of practical ability
    (a) Sales department: 20 days/month × 8 hours/day × 60 minutes × 12 persons = 115,200 minutes
    (b) Production control department: 20 days/month × 8 hours/day × 60 minutes × 2 persons = 19,200 minutes
(4) Capacity cost rate
    Capacity cost rate = department cost/practical working hours
    (a) Capacity cost rate of the sales department = 748,800/115,200 = 6.5 dollars/minute
    (b) Capacity cost rate of the production control department = 96,000/19,200 = 5 dollars/minute
(5) Number of accepted orders
    A-order = 10,000
    B-order = 1,000

Process cost and the used and unused capacity can be calculated as shown in Table 1 based on the virtual example above.

Panel A shows calculation results using Kaplan & Anderson's (2004) method (process cost by TD-ABC). This result is based on standard activity time, disregarding the stay time between activities or processes (core processes). As a result, the unused capacity rate of the sales department is 52.2%, as shown in panel A, and the unused capacity rate of the production control department is 58.3%.

On the other hand, if input time and output time are measured for each department according to each order, it is possible to understand and use the total processing time for A- and B-orders by department. In other words, if the total activity time for an A-order is 62,500 minutes, the total activity time for B-orders with 6,000 minutes for the sales department and 9,000 minutes for the production control department yields an unused capacity rate different from that in panel A. Panel B reports the results of this separate calculation, in which the unused capacity rates are 40.5% and 53.1% for the sales department and production control department,

Table 1.   Process cost by TD-ABC and PO-ABC

Panel A: Process cost by TD-ABC

Order	Department	Core process	Unit time number of orders	Cost per hour ($)	Total activity time of core process (minutes)	Total cost ($)
A-Order	Sales	Negotiation process	2 minutes	6.5	20,000	130,000
		Order process	3 minutes	6.5	30,000	195,000
		Total orders accepted	10,000 order			325,000
B-Order	Sales	Negotiation process	2 minutes	6.5	2,000	13,000
		Order process	3 minutes	6.5	3,000	19,500
	Production control	Customize plan process	5 minutes	5	5,000	25,000
		Prat purchase process	3 minutes	5	3,000	15,000
		Total orders accepted	1,000 order			72,500
Used capacity of sales department					55,000	357,500**
Unused capacity					60,200	391,300***
Unused capacity ratio					52.2%*	52.2%
Total of sales department					115,200	748,800
Used capacity of production control department					8,000	40,000****
Unused capacity					11,200	56,000
Unused capacity ratio					58.3%	58.3%
Total of production control					19,200	96,000

*52.2% = (60,200/115,200) × 100

**357,500 = Allocated cost to core process for A- and B-orders from the sales department
= 325,000 + (13,000 + 19,500)

***391,300 = Total cost of sales department – Allocated cost to core process for A- and B-orders from the sales department
= 748,800 – 357,500

****40,000 = Allocated cost to core process for B-order for the production control department
= 25,000 + 15,000

(Continued)

Table 1. *(Continued)*

Panel B: Process cost by PO-ABC

Order	Department	Core process	Unit time number of order	Cost per hour ($)	Total activity time of core process (minutes)	Total activity time of mega process (minutes)	Total cost ($)
A-Order	Sales	Negotiation process	2 minutes	6.5	20,000		130,000
		Order process	3 minutes	6.5	30,000		195,000
		Total orders accepted	10,000 order				325,000
						62,500	406,250*
B-Order	Sales	Negotiation process	2 minutes	6.5	2,000		13,000
		Order process	3 minutes	6.5	3,000		19,500
						6,000	39,000
	Production control	Customize plan process	5 minutes	5	5,000		25,000
		Prat purchase process	3 minutes	5	3,000		15,000
		Total orders accepted	1,000 order				72,500
						9,000	45,000**
Used capacity of sales department		Core process			55,000		357,500
		Mega process				68,500	445,250***
Unused capacity					60,200	46,700	303,550
Unused capacity ratio					52.2%	40.5%	40.5%****
		Total of sales department			115,200	115,200	748,800

Used capacity of production control department	Core process	8,000		40,000
	Mega process		9,000	45,000
Unused capacity		11,200	10,200	51,000
Unused capacity ratio		58.3%	53.1%	53.1%
Total of production control		19,200	19,200	96,000

*406,250 = Allocated cost to mega process by A-order of sales department
  $= 6.5 \times 62,500$

**45,000 = Allocated cost, mega process for B-orders for the production control department
  $= 5 \times 9,000$

***445,250 = Allocated cost, mega process for all order for the sales department
  = Allocated cost, mega process by A- and B-orders for the sales department
  $= 406,250 + 39,000$

****40.5% $= (303,550/748,800) \times 100$

respectively. This yields differences of 11.7% (52.2–40.5%) and 5.2% (58.3–53.1%) for the sales and production departments, respectively, compared to panel A. This depends on the differences in the total activity time between the mega process and core process, which represents stay time, which TD-ABC does not account for. In other words, the PO-ABC method with processes in a hierarchical structure proposed in this Paper shows the 11.7% of capacity used in the sales department's stay time. This is useful as basic data for process improvement.

5. Comparison of TD-ABC and BPM/PO-ABC

Several differences become clear from the above comparison of the PO-ABC method proposed in this study to Kaplan & Anderson's (2004) TD-ABC method.

(1) PO-ABC can calculate stay time and cost for sub-processes by layering the processes (for example, mega process → core process).
(2) The unused capacity in Kaplan & Anderson (2004) is inaccurate because it includes the stay time between activities or processes.
(3) In PO-ABC, the time equation is unnecessary because the process used time can be calculated for each order.
(4) BPM is relatively easy in today's IT environment. If BPM is available, activity time and process used time can be measured automatically. This means that there are few errors in the time measurements.
(5) Similar orders may have different activity time and process used time in PO-ABC. However, if a large time lag appears, the cause can be pursued as management by exception.

6. Conclusion

Nearly 30 years have passed since Kaplan proposed the original ABC/ABM. However, the business community did not have a big reaction and its use in practice is rather low. There are feasibility problems in ABC, which Kaplan & Anderson (2004, 2007a) identified to explain the low utilization. In addition, some factors inhibit the diffusion of ABC, which were mentioned in the introduction of this paper.

This study compared the characteristic of TD-ABC to the conventional ABC method in terms of feasibility. In addition, the potential to integrate process improvement was discussed in terms of the usefulness of the proposed PO-ABC/BPM method.

This study analyzed two problems in TD-ABC. First, Kaplan & Anderson (2004) assume that the process is given as the chain of activities, and take this assumption as the basis of TD-ABC. However, in practice, many companies do not construct process or a suitable management system. It is very difficult to construct and control processes. This is because a company must create a structure to control process performance by matching processes with changes in the environment. This paper indicated that it is possible to improve processes and the utility value by applying PO-ABC after implementing BPM to control processes.

Kaplan & Anderson (2004) argued that TD-ABC is superior to conventional ABC because of its useful measurement of process used time and time equations. However, it does not consider the stay time between activities or processes and includes it in the unused capacity in their method. In other words, TD-ABC has a structure that makes it hard to connect to process improvement if the company should consider stay time.

This study clearly mentioned that controlling processes for each order after mapping the process structure using BPM is very useful in improving processes by automatically measuring the process used time for each order. The time equation is not necessary. In addition, this study demonstrated that a useful cost accounting and cost management system can be constructed by combining BPM and PO-ABC, which can help companies improve a cycle because it can unify the management accounting technique and the field management technique by confirming and improving capacity, time, and cost using a simulation.

References

Askarany, D. & Smith, M. (2004). Contextual Factors and Administrative Changes. *Journal of Issues in Informing Science and Information Technology,* Vol. 1, pp. 179–188.

Askarany, D. & Yazdifar, H. (2007). Why ABC Is Not Widely Implemented? *International Journal of Business Research,* Vol. 7, No.1, pp. 93–98.

Castellano, J. F., Young S., Anderson D. & Mclean, W. (2004). Process-based Measurements: The Key to More Effective Decision Making, *Cost Management*, pp. 5–14.

Innes, J., Mitchell, F. & Sinclair, D. (2000). Activity-based Costing in the U.K.'s Largest Companies: A Comparison of 1994 and 1999 Survey Results, *Management Accounting Research*, Vol. 11, No. 3, pp. 349–362.

Johnson, H. T. & Kaplan, R. S. (1987). *Relevance Lost: The Rise and Fall of Management Accounting*, Harvard Business School Press.

Kaplan, R. S. & Anderson, S. R. (2004). Time-driven Activity-based Costing, *Harvard Business Review*, pp. 131–138.

Kaplan, R. S. & Anderson, S. R. (2007a). *Time-driven Activity-based Costing*, Harvard Business School Press.

Kaplan, R. S. & Anderson, S. R. (2007b). The Innovation of Time-driven Activity-based Costing, *Cost Management*, pp. 5–15.

Keys, D. E. & Lefevre, R. J. (1995). Departmental Activity-based Management, *Management Accounting*, pp. 27–30.

Kim, S., Lee, G. & Kim, T. (1996). The Departmental Activity-based Costing System of a Korean Company: The Case of Anam Industrial Co., Ltd., *The Japanese Association of Management Accounting*, Vol. 4, No. 1, pp. 59–76 (in Japanese).

Lawson, R. A. (1994). Beyond ABC: Process-based Costing, *Journal of Cost Management*, pp. 33–43.

Moinuddin, K., Collins, T. & Bansal, A. (2007). Process Activity Mapping: Activity-Based Costing for Semiconductor Enterprises, *Cost Management*, pp. 29–33.

Ness, J. A. & Cucuzza, T. G. (1995). Tapping the Full Potential of ABC, *Harvard Business Review*, pp. 130–138.

Nippon University, Department of Commercial Science, Accounting Research Institute. (2004). The Construction of the General Database of Cost Accounting, the Management Accounting Practice, *Accounting Research*, No. 17, pp. 147–150 (in Japanese).

Tanaka, T. (1993). The Theory Structure of Activity Accounts and the Usefulness Accounts, Accounting, *Moriyama Shoten*, Vol. 143, No. 6, pp. 1–19 (in Japanese).

An Application of the Most Effective KPI in Business Management — Development and Application of KPI Pool

Kenji Hirayama
President & CEO, Gimbal LLC, Japan

Yoshiyuki Nagasaka
Professor, Konan University, Japan

1. Introduction

In business management, indicator is an easily decipherable measure of business performance that is based on the analysis of financial statements, such as income statement, balance sheet, and cash-flow statements. Concerning analysis and the practical use of financial statements, many studies are accomplished and are inflected in the management of an enterprise routinely (Sakurai, 2012).

In addition, alongside Investor Relations (IR) activity, companies continuously improve financial analysis and disclosure standards to communicate effectively with the investors and shareholders. In addition, an improvement activity linking financial and non-financial information ("consolidated information") can be presented in a comparable format to attract the attention of the stakeholders (Ichimura, 2013).

The international body responsible for the consolidation of information, International Integrated Reporting Council (IIRC), builds the framework for the consolidation of reports. The activity of developing contents for "business results" that constitute the consolidated information focuses on the manner in which the Key Performance Indicators (KPIs), qualitative and quantitative, achieve the strategic objectives and overall management strategy of a company.

On the other hand, the financial performance indicators implemented to measure management performance are developed in each company through innovative ideas (Donald & Richards, 1986; David, 2010).

While KPIs are set to monitor a management activity, particularly an important indicator, Key Goal Indicators (KGIs) show the performance of a management activity. KGIs frequently use measures like "amount of sales" and "operating earning rate" to measure management performance, whereas KPI measures the "number of inquiries", "number of customer calls", "yield percentage", and "number of claims" for a certain period to manage the business management activity (Kaplan & Norton, 1992, 2001). However, in 1995, the continuous improvement activities such as the quality control (QC) activities were carried out lively in Japan, and there were few companies that understood the concept of managing business using the KPI measures (KPI management) (Hronec, 1994).

The collapse of the bubble economy in Japan negatively affected the business results of Nissan Motor Co., Ltd. The company witnessed a decline in the management performance and invited Carlos Ghosn of Renault S.A.S to take over the management as the CEO & President in 1999. When President Carlos Ghosn made repeated use of the word "commitment" during a press conference for the announcement of the business plan, it came to be understood that it is a business management method to clarify KPIs and commit to their achievement. In other words, during the press conference, "KPI was made clear, and the achievement of the business objective was committed" across the organization. As the KPI management improved the management performance in Nissan Motor, many Japanese enterprises and consulting firms came to pay big concern to KPI management. Carlos Ghosn gives a presentation on the business approach in his book (Carlos, 2001).

The three basic indicators are Q (Quality), C (Cost), and D (Delivery), and are commonly recognized as the most important indicators by the executive management of the manufacturing industry. If manufacturing costs increase in the course of improving the quality of a product, and the activity consequently increases the turnaround time, then the product loses its competitive edge in the market. Therefore, a high-level reciprocity indicator should be achieved for measuring management performance by setting the indicator in a manner similar to that of the QCD system. This indicator is referred to as sales target and profit goal. In addition, it is important to undertake activities for improving performance using the indicator. This shows the importance of adopting the practice of "management by KPI" in business management. However, it is not easy to balance the application of the most effective KPIs.

This paper considers the balanced application of the most effective KPIs in business management. First, about the application of KPI, a method performed for applying KPI was introduced. The validity of the method was analyzed based on the findings of the KPI application to a real-time business re-engineering project.

When the person in charge of applying the KPIs performs the application, the method facilitates the application of the most effective KPI by providing the person in charge a framework for thinking. However, it is not expected that the application of effective KPIs surpass the knowledge and the wisdom of the person performing the method. The thought of the person in charge of the application can be widened by providing knowledge, thereby equipping the person to apply the most effective KPI. Therefore, the limitation of performing this method can be overcome by providing organizational support for broadening the thinking of the person in charge.

Specifically, a wide range of KPIs was collected from various materials and organized. In addition, 1,697 KPIs were arranged in a predetermined format, and a KPI Pool was developed for supporting the application of the most effective KPI. It is understood that an organization moves in direction to achieve the KPI objectives. Therefore, it is thought that the objective of organization can be accomplished more reasonably by applying KPIs that are most effective in achieving these objectives.

KPI Pool was applied to the business process re-engineering project in a company. In addition, it was confirmed that the KPI Pool could be used practically by applying the most effective KPI. This paper introduces a business process re-engineering project case study that utilized the KPI

Pool in an SCM project of a company producing small- to middle-sized liquid crystals.

2. Issues in Performing the Method of KPI Application

To date, various methods have been developed for supporting the extraction and application of the most effective KPI. The three methods that were applied to the real business process re-engineering project and business management re-engineering project are introduced and the issue with each of these methods is discussed. The three methods are as follows:

(1) "4 × 3 matrix"
(2) "Five viewpoints"
(3) "not go well vs. goes well"

Positioning and articulation of the three methods that were performed for the application of KPI are shown in Fig. 1. The high-end framework in Fig. 1 has the potential to produce the most effective output KPIs. Each person in charge who showed it in the first framework does not master business in many cases. Therefore, a method to support the extraction and application of KPI was developed and shown in the second frame and has been considered as a practical method for utilization in a business.

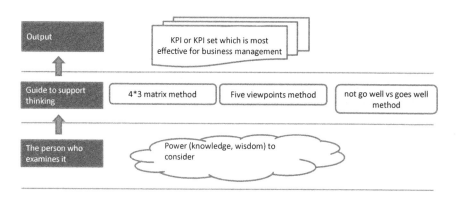

Fig. 1.   Positioning and articulation of the method performed for the application of KPI

2.1. KPI application and application issue using the "4 × 3 matrix" method

The evaluation of achievement in the manufacturing department using KPIs is exemplified in Fig. 2. The KPIs are applied in the 12 quadrants using "4 × 3 matrix". The four classes of the balanced scorecard (BSC) are distributed along the y-axis, and the x-axis shows three categories of QCD, which "include the three manufacturing principles", and the most effective KPI is considered in the framework of 12 total quadrants.

KPI is considered from a broader perspective by focusing on the four classes of BSC, and the most effective KPI is applied. In addition, dividing the KPIs under three separate QCD categories facilitates an easy understanding of KPIs that are applied to each area of business management (Hronec, 1994).

The person in charge extracts more KPI candidates by using the framework of 12 quadrants and can apply the most effective KPI from the

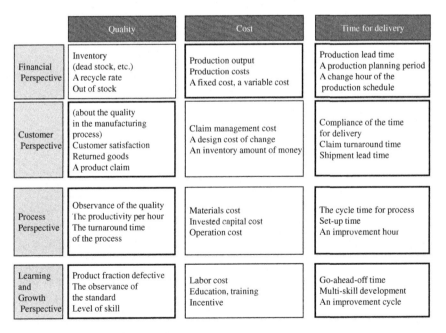

	Quality	Cost	Time for delivery
Financial Perspective	Inventory (dead stock, etc.) A recycle rate Out of stock	Production output Production costs A fixed cost, a variable cost	Production lead time A production planning period A change hour of the production schedule
Customer Perspective	(about the quality in the manufacturing process) Customer satisfaction Returned goods A product claim	Claim management cost A design cost of change An inventory amount of money	Compliance of the time for delivery Claim turnaround time Shipment lead time
Process Perspective	Observance of the quality The productivity per hour The turnaround time of the process	Materials cost Invested capital cost Operation cost	The cycle time for process Set-up time An improvement hour
Learning and Growth Perspective	Product fraction defective The observance of the standard Level of skill	Labor cost Education, training Incentive	Go-ahead-off time Multi-skill development An improvement cycle

Fig. 2. An example of the "4 × 3 matrix" method (KPI for performance evaluation of the manufacturing departments)

extracted KPIs. However, the problem of this method is that the extraction of the most effective KPI is limited to the knowledge and wisdom of the person in charge of the extraction (cf. Fig. 1). It implies that the most effective KPI candidate is not extracted due to the limited business knowledge of the person in charge, although the person uses the framework of 12 quadrants.

2.2. *KPI application and application issue of using the "five viewpoints method"*

"Five viewpoints method" is developed to enable an inexperienced person to extract KPI, and thereby overcome the issue of the "4 × 3 matrix method." In this method, the five most important viewpoints that can be employed practically in the business of management consulting are used for KPI application.

The five viewpoints are mentioned below, and a summary of the "five viewpoints method" is shown in Fig. 3.

(1) A calculating formula
(2) Mutual relation
(3) Constraints
(4) A representative value or alternative feature
(5) Direction of the change

This method provides a viewpoint to the person in charge, but is not cyclopedic. A person who possesses a good understanding of the business can only extract the most effective KPI. It is hard to extract KPI showing the direction of the changes, such as "the percentages of women managers", by the "4 × 3 matrix method". However, the person in charge extracts several KPIs and applies the most effective KPI during an examination of the fifth viewpoint to "show the direction of the change". However, the issue with the application of this method for the extraction of KPI is that it is limited to the field of experience and knowledge of the person in charge. Wide knowledge and wisdom based on the experience are necessary in the extraction of balanced KPIs.

A name	Definition	An example	A characteristic
1. A calculating formula	The indicator is shown in a calculating formula, and a constituent of the calculating formula is KPI candidate	The increase of the gross margin in the case of an example (1) Sales = product unit price × unit sales (2) Gross margin = (product unit price − product cost) × unit sales For the increase of the gross margin, sales, unit price, unit sales, cost become targeted for examination of KPI	The indicator about figure and the production of financial statements is defined by a concrete calculating formula. Therefore, concrete management indicator becomes the KPI candidate by indicator being described in a calculating formula.
2. Mutual relation	Conflicting indicator is extracted as a set by expressing mutual relation between the indicators	In a door-to-door sales activity, the increase of the number of new clients can be accomplished by "an increase of the number of new visits" and "the quality improvement of the visit activity". increase of the number of new clients = "increase of the number of new visits " × "quality improvement of the visit activity"	Each is KPI, but there is generally negative correlation between these two activities. In this way, KPI is extracted by mutual relation.

(Continued)

A name	Definition	An example	A characteristic
3. Constraints	Constraint is stunting in the achievement of purpose. And the constraint is considered as KPI.	The production capacity of operation having lowest production capacity is set in KPI on increasing output of the whole productive process. Productivity of the whole productive process raises it by improving production capacity of the constraint operation.	There is various constraint such as the constraint of the financial resources credit, constraint of the production capacity, constraint of the human ability, and KPI is considered for constraint for these.
4. "A representative value" or "alternative characteristic"	The whole process is managed in some representative values or alternative characteristic. The representative value or alternative characteristic is considered as KPI.	For example, by the manufacturing process of the semiconductor, the utilization rate of the whole manufacturing process is judged from utilization rate of "the exposure machine" which is a representative production equipment.	According to "the principle of 20:80", the whole is almost grasped in a representative value extracted reasonably. For example, it is a representative product, main manufacturing process, a main client.
5. A direction of the change	Indicator showing the direction of the change becomes the driving force of the realization of the change.	For example, it is the indicator with the impact KPI that "the manager percentage of the woman becomes 30% in five years" is concrete, and to show the direction of the change now when the manager percentage of the woman is 10%	The direction of the change is often described by abstract words. The image of the change is shown as a concrete activity by setting KPI showing the direction of the change.

Fig. 3.   The summary of "five viewpoints" method (five viewpoints, definition, example, and characteristics)

2.3. KPI application and application issue of KPI using the "not go well vs. goes well" method

A gap between the current condition of an organization and the ideal state indicates a problem. In that case, a business improvement activity is undertaken to solve the problem and achieve the ideal state (Kuridani, 2012). Therefore, the question, "what kind of conditions are good?" is repeated in a business improvement activity. Furthermore, the question, "what kind of indicator measures the good conditions?" also forms a part of the activity. The repetitive employment of these questions throughout the activity led to the extraction of the most effective KPI. In addition, the question "what kind of conditions are bad?" is repeated. Furthermore, the question, "what kind of indicator measures the bad condition?" facilitates the extraction of several KPIs during the activity.

KPI is extracted widely by examining a problem state as well as a good state. The most effective KPI is applied from the KPI candidate that is extracted as a result of these interactive questions. This method is called "not go well vs. goes well method". Fig. 4 provides an example of extracting KPI for production management activities using the "not go well vs. goes well method". The phrase "a lot of Indicators" in Fig. 4 is as KPI candidate extracted as a result of interactive question. The most effective KPI is applied while deliberating on the cause-and-effect relationship among the indicators given in the list of "a lot of Indicators". When applied KPI turns worse in the practical business, as for the cause, it is studied as cause as the Indicator which is related while thinking about cause-and-effect relationships from "a lot of Indicators".

When the most effective person possessing a strong business understanding is chosen to extract the KPIs by this method, the KPIs that accord with actualities are extracted and the most effective KPI is applied. However, similar to the "4 × 3 matrix" and "five viewpoints" methods, a person with lesser abilities and experience fails to extract enough KPIs using this method. However, this method facilitates the extraction of a broad range of KPIs and the application of the most effective KPI when an expert consultant possessing a practical understanding of the business and the ability to ask precise questions is given the responsibility of extracting the KPIs.

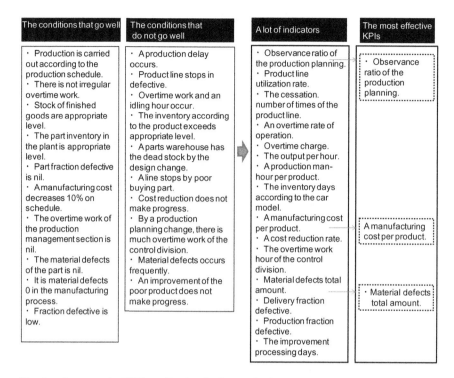

Fig. 4.   An example (KPI application in the production management activity) using the "not go well vs. goes well" method

3. Method to Support Application of the Most Effective KPI by the Development of a KPI Pool

3.1. *What is KPI Pool?*

The use of this method can facilitate extraction and application of a broad range of KPIs by giving the person in charge "a framework for thought". However, this method cannot extract the most effective KPI, as the extraction is limited to the knowledge and the wisdom of the person in charge. If the person in charge of extraction is provided knowledge, then the person broadens thought patterns and the ideas using the knowledge. This will enable the person in charge to reflect deeply on the most effective KPIs and move beyond existing boundaries of knowledge and the wisdom to extract the most effective KPIs.

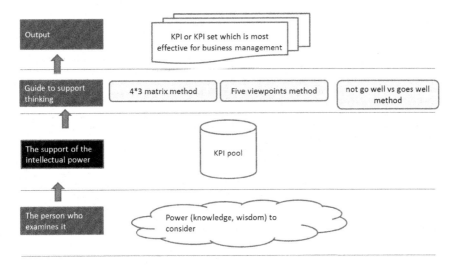

Fig. 5. The framework for the application of KPI using the KPI Pool

Therefore, the author collected various KPIs from various materials and selected a total of 1,697 KPIs to form the KPI Pool. The framework for the application of KPI using the KPI Pool is shown in Fig. 5.

The following three elements are necessary for the KPI Pool:

(1) Collected KPIs are actually used in business politics.
(2) KPI candidates are extracted from the collected KPI.
(3) Related information to support the thought of the person in charge is included in KPI.

A concrete explanation on the KPI Pool is provided in the following section.

3.2. *Arrangement of the KPI Pool*

Several KPIs were extracted from materials prepared for the client project, literature (including a magazine on business politics), and materials from websites to form the KPI Pool. The KPI Pool was arranged in an Excel worksheet, and the number of KPIs totaled to 1,697. The layout of the KPI Pool is shown in Fig. 6.

① Financial	Customer	Process	Learning and growth	② Category	③ Indicator NO.	④ Indicator name	⑤ Summary (definition) of the indicator
o	o	o		1.increase of the sales	a01001	The profit ratio via Internet among gross returns	
o	o			1.Increase of	a01002	Sales ranking according	Sales conditions

⑥ Footnote	⑦ Indicator calculating formula	⑧ Strategy	⑨ Tactics examples
The increase of the sales amount on the Internet reduces sale overhead expense and helps collection of client information.		Sales enlargement (growth) strategy (A01), cost reduction strategy (A02), commercial value improvement strategy (B01), accompaniment service value improvement strategy (B02), correspondence/ support power improvement strategy (B03), enclosure strategy (B04), product planning, development, design (C02), business development and sale (C05).	(A01) Collection of client information. (A02) Reduction of the sales cost. (B01)) The convenience improvement of the client. (B02)) Increase of the sales opportunities on the Internet. (B03) Increase of the sale on the Internet. (B04)) The convenience improvement of the client, collection of client information. (C02) The convenience improvement of the client. (C05) Increase of the sales opportunities on the Internet, reduction of the sales cost, collection of client information
		Sales enlargement (growth) strategy (A01), enclosure strategy (B04), business development and sale (C05).	(A01) The increase of sales, the enlargement of the share in the client. (B04)) The enlargement of the share in the client. (C05)) The enlargement of the share in the client
		Sales enlargement (growth) strategy (A01), business development and sales (C05).	(A01) The increase of sales, enlargement of the marketshare. (C05)) Enlargement of the marketshare
The increase of the sales amount on the Internet reduces sale overhead expense and helps collection of client information. It expresses the purchasing behavior of the client. Furthermore, the comparison with the company of the same category does not depend on the size of enterprise.	Sales growth rate in comparison with the competitor = A company's sales growth rate ÷ The sales growth rate of the competitor	Sales enlargement (growth) strategy (A01), innovation strategy (C01), product planning, development, design (C02), business development and sales (C05), strategic clarification (D04).	(A01) The increase of sales, enlargement of the marketshare. (C01)) Product leadership. (C02)) Product leadership. (C05)) Enlargement of the marketshare. (D04)) Product leadership.
	Net sales revenue = "sales" − "sales drawback" − "rebate" (a discount).	Sales enlargement (growth) strategy (A01).	(A01) The increase of sales.

Fig. 6.   Layout of KPI Pool

There are four columns in Fig. 6. ⑦ is distributed between four classes of BSC — finance, client, process, learning and growth. A total of 478 KPIs is stored in the "finance" column. The "category" column comprises nine items including an increase in the sales, an improvement in the shareholder value, an improvement in the client share, cost reduction, finance stability, an increase in profit, the maximum practical use of holding assets, an appropriate and practical use of holding assets, and increases in earnings. Each KPI and each category are arranged in relation to 1:1.

A total of 225 KPIs is stored in the "clients" column. The category is composed of nine items including an increase in the sales, business strategy; customer relationship, acquisition of client information, client retention, client acquisition, and customer satisfaction; product leadership; and improved qualities. Each KPI and each category are arranged in relation to 1:1.

The "process" column has 719 KPIs. The category is composed of six items including the practical use of IT, business development, business operation, cost management, cost reduction, and facilities management. Each KPI and each category are arranged concerning 1:1.

A total of 257 KPIs is stored in the "learning and growth" column. The category is composed of six items including research and development, talent management, technology, information, the practical use of intangible assets, and organizational culture. Each KPI and each category are arranged concerning 1:1.

As for Fig. 6 ⑧: strategies, all of the 1,697 KPIs are related to strategies. The number of strategies was finally reduced to 21 by an inductive method. Plural strategies are related to one KPI. Therefore, the KPI and the strategic name are expressed as "1: N".

As for Fig. 6 ⑨: tactics, all of the 1,697 KPIs are related to tactics. Tactics necessary to achieve each KPI was considered and listed. The tactics were arranged by an inductive method, and the number of tactics was finally reduced to 738. Subsequently, the relationship between 738 tactics and each KPI was established. Plural tactics are related to one KPI. Therefore, the KPI and the tactics name are expressed as "1: N". As a result, a relationship between the tactics and strategies was established in the KPI Pool through the KPIs. A few tactics carry out the strategy. Therefore, a strategic achievement level is measured in the applied KPI, and it is measured by KPI where the execution level of the tactics was applied to. In this way, strategy, tactics, and KPI are simultaneously considered by the KPI Pool.

3.3. *Extraction of the KPI candidate using search feature and the filter function of Excel*

The person involved in the extraction of KPI can extract plural KPI candidates using search feature and the filter function of Excel. The most effective KPI is chosen among the extracted KPI candidates depending on a purpose.

The risk of extracting only intelligible KPIs defined by the project's members, such as "turnover of inventories" and "dead stock" is analyzed, when the person responsible for KPI extraction is deputed among the finance and accounting members of a project to manage inventory reduction. However, it is extracted as "the KPI candidate of the client's viewpoint" — "out-of-stock rate" or "stock inquiry time" — when the KPI Pool is utilized. Therefore, the project member recognizes that the improvement in "the time for delivery observance rate" is necessary with a reduction in inventory. This facilitates the establishment of the most effective KPI for business management.

However, the most effective KPI candidate is not always extracted from the KPI Pool. The number of KPI accumulated in the KPI Pool is 1,697, and not all the KPIs are covered in the pool. The KPI Pool supports the thinking of the person in charge of extracting the KPI candidates.

4. Business Process Re-Engineering by KPI Pool

4.1. *Practical use of KPI pool in a liquid crystalline manufacturing company*

Hitachi Displays Co., Ltd. (existing: Japan Display Inc.) was responsible for the liquid crystalline business in a subsidiary of Hitachi Ltd. The company is a global player that is engaged in the development, production, and sales of small liquid crystals for use in cell phones. In Hitachi Displays Co., Ltd., a performance management re-engineering project was carried out from 2004 to 2007 (Hirayama *et al.*, 2014).

As for the action, the information between work fronts is related to business politics in KPI, and it is a building activity of the mechanism of the business management that plan–do–check–action (PDCA) cycle turns around monthly.

(1) Drawing up of the "strategy map"

The company mainly produces a liquid crystalline unit for cell phones. The ability of the business to turn development, manufacturing, and supply in a short term has contributed to its success. The "strategy map" was made by a project member for setting KPIs, which was a critical need for enhancing the effectiveness of business management.

The y-axis of "strategy map" has four classes of BSC and the x-axis shows four business processes including "sales, development, production, and supply". The most effective KPI is considered in the framework of 16 total quadrants. In addition, the critical KPIs for all business processes were extracted.

The following activities were mainly carried out for the extraction of the KPI candidates:

① The KPI candidates were extracted from a real business report of the company.

② Associated KPIs between business processes were extracted with reference to KPI which is before and after business processes. For example, production planning data and actual production data are necessary for "inventory management". Shipment plan data and shipment achievement data are necessary for collating business processes information on sales.

③ The KPI candidate considered to be effective was extracted using the character search feature of the KPI Pool.

A part of the "strategy map" drawn up in this way is shown in Fig. 7. The Enterprise Resource Planning (ERP) of a global major is adopted for all business processes including sales, purchase, production, physical distribution, and accounting. In addition, an Manufacturing Execution System (MES) was introduced into production field, and a mechanism was built for "business management by IT". Therefore, as a basic policy in the applications of KPI, all applied KPIs were extracted from an ERP system and submitted.

A total of 341 applied KPIs were finally extracted from an ERP system and listed in a business report. KPI that is newly applied using the KPI Pool was around 10% of the 341 applied KPIs. The company was able to add important KPIs by using the KPI pool.

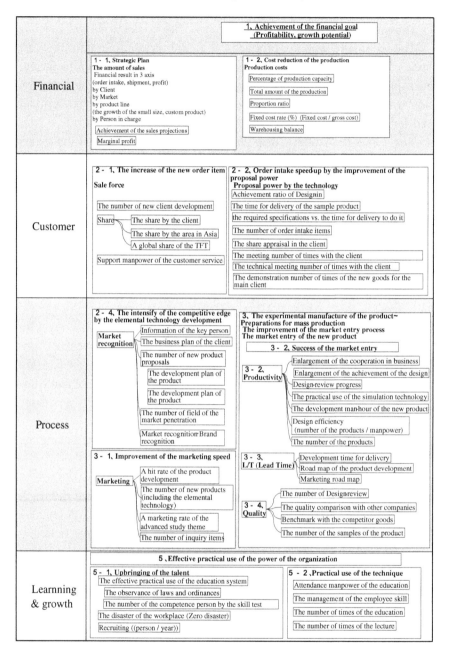

Fig. 7.   "Strategy map" of the small liquid crystalline manufacturing company (a part, an extract)

Table. 1   The number of KPIs in the scorecard

No	Breadown of KPI	Level 0	Level 1	Level 2	Level 3	Level 4	Level 5	Level 6	Total
		No. of KPI	No. of KPI	No. of KPI	No. of KPI	No. of KPI	No. of KPI	No. of KPI	No. of KPI
1	Financial	1	6	13	1	0	0	0	21
2	Client (Brand) * 1	1	4	5	20	21	0	0	51
3	Process (Brand) * 1	0	2	2	3	5	4	0	16
4	Process (By Production) * 2	1	4	14	24	32	1	0	76
5	Process (SCM)	1	1	2	5	17	103	32	161
6	Fundamental technology	1	3	6	2	4	0	0	16
	Total	5	20	42	55	79	108	32	341

(1*) The indicato which evaluates the value of the client.

(2*) E.g. Designer productivity, production engineer productivity.

In the indicator of 39 items chosen from level 1,2,3 reported in a monthly business meeting.

Level 2: It is reported in a business meeting once in a quarter by each department.

Level 3: It is reported once for one year by each department.

(2) Business management by organized and practical use of KPI

KPI is appropriately used in an administrative action when it is submitted by "a person who needs KPI and can use KPI for business management" (PDCA) (with responsibility and the authority). Therefore, as for the y-axis of the "scorecard", a management stratum with seven classes from level 0 to level 6 was designed. The x-axis shows six items including finance, a client (Brand), a process (Brand), a process (By Production), a process (SCM), and Fundamental technology. In addition, the most effective KPI was applied in framework of total 42 quadrants. The business meeting is held to provide monthly, quarterly, and annual report on KPI usage. The number of classified KPI is shown in Table. 1.

5. Summary

In business management, the practice of "management by KPI" has gained significance. However, the application of balanced and most effective KPI is not easy. This paper considered the application of important balanced and most effective KPIs in business management. First, about an application of KPI, a method was introduced, and the validity of the method was evaluated from the result that applied the method to a real business re-engineering project. The performance of the method will facilitate application of a broad range of effective KPIs by giving the person in charge the framework of thinking. However, it is not expected that the extraction of most effective KPI would surpass the knowledge and the wisdom of the person responsible for KPI extraction.

Therefore, the provision of knowledge can broaden the thoughts of the extractor. This will enable the person responsible for extraction to reflect deeply and apply the most effective KPI. The limitations of the performance of the method can be overcome by providing organizational support to the thinking of the person in charge.

Specifically, various KPIs were collected and organized using various materials. In addition, 1,697 KPIs were finally selected in a predetermined format, and a KPI Pool was developed for supporting the application of the most effective KPI. The KPI Pool was applied to the business process re-engineering project of company. In addition, it was confirmed that the practical use of KPI Pool was useful for the application of the most effective KPI. This paper introduced the business process re-engineering project case study that utilized the KPI Pool in an SCM project of a company producing small- to middle-sized liquid crystals. Through a lot more practice, an application method for the most effective KPI is developed and can be applied to business process re-engineering projects in future.

References

Carlos, G. (2001). *Renaissance*, DIAMOND Inc. (in Japanese).

David, P. (2010). *Key Performance Indicators (KPI): Developing, Implementing, and Using Winning KPIs*, 2nd Edition, John Wiley & Sons.

Donald, K. C. & Richards, E. C. (1986). *Winning Performance*, *PRESIDENT* Inc. (in Japanese).

Hirayama, K., Yano, T. & Nagasaka, Y. (2014). Business Improvement Projects using Key Performance Indicator, *KONAN BI Monograph*, Series No. 2014-001 Financia.

Hronec, S. M. (1994). *Vital signs*, Arthur Andersen & Co., SANNO Institute of Management Publication dept. (in Japanese).

Ichimura, K, Ernst, & Young ShinNihon LLC. (2013). *Implementing Integrated Reporting*, Dai-ichi Hoki, Co, Ltd. (in Japanese).

Kaplan, R. S. & Norton, D. P. (1992). The Balanced Scorecard: Measures that Drive Performance, *Harvard Business Review*, pp. 71–80.

Kaplan, R. S. & Norton, D. P. (2001). *The Strategy-Focused Organization*, Toyo Keizai Inc. (in Japanese).

Sakurai, H. (2012). *Financial Statement Analysis*, Chuokeizai-sha Holdings Inc. (in Japanese).

Toyota Production System for Business Process Management

Noriyuki Imai
Part-time Professor, Graduate School of Business,
Meijo University

1. Introduction

Approximately a century has passed since Taylor (1911) proposed a system of scientific management and Ford (1922) introduced his mass-production system during the Second Industrial Revolution. Productivity improvement has remained a constant business management issue as industrial society developed throughout the intervening years. Although many techniques to improve productivity have been conceived and practiced in various locations and industries throughout the world, this paper will focus on the Toyota Production System (TPS) created in Japan.

The TPS, developed and implemented by the Toyota company to improve productivity, is one of the most famous Japanese production models. It strengthened the international competitiveness of a wide range of Japanese manufacturing industries by improving productivity, greatly contributing to Japan's economic development.

However, strategic management theory flourishes in the current business environment. The mature TPS is shifting from productivity improvements in manufacturing processes to focus more on customer-oriented, cross-sectional Business Process Management (BPM) to increase adaptability to customer needs by offering diversified, high-quality products with minimal lead time.

This paper will examine the use of TPS for BPM from three perspectives. We will first describe the historical arc of the changes to and evolution of the TPS. Second, we consider how TPS techniques can increase adaptability to customer needs. Finally, we apply the manufacturability viewpoint and the environmental and accounting viewpoints to investigate prospects for further evolution in the TPS.

Most of this paper's content is based on the author's knowledge and experience gained by working in the automotive industry. Additionally, "Toyota" as used in this paper refers to the Toyota Group generally; we will not consider cases of its individual businesses.

2. The TPS as a Means to Improve Productivity

The TPS was developed and implemented by the Toyota company to improve productivity and is one of the most famous Japanese production models.

Ohno (1978) states that the TPS is a production method resulting from many years of trial and error by Toyota after World War II as it shouldered the fate of Japan's automotive industry. By this, Ohno (1978) meant that it had to survive competition with the established mass-production systems of the Western automotive industries, without funds or state-of-the-art facilities, and within the constraints of a Japanese automotive market that called for small-lot production of a wide variety of products.

Western mass-production systems were upstream to downstream systems, also known as push systems, where models were successively turned into manufactured goods. According to Ohno (1978), the Western automotive industry often used the term "Maxcy–Silberston curve" (Maxcy & Silberston, 1959). This principle of volume efficiency, where an increase in production volume leads to a marked and proportionate reduction in the cost of each automobile, was proven in the high economic growth that continued until 1973, and it became deeply ingrained in the minds of those involved in the Western automotive industry.

Toyota, on the other hand, began thinking around 1950 that blindly imitating Ford's mass-production system was dangerous. Therefore, it stressed that the goal of the TPS, building on the ideals of successive

Toyota executives, was to improve productivity and reduce costs by thoroughly eliminating all forms of *muda* (waste) from its plants. Monden (2006) states that the ultimate goal of the TPS is to augment the company's profits as a whole by increasing productivity and reducing costs by eliminating excessive workforces, facilities, and inventory.

According to Monden (2006), the chain of *muda* results from excessive production resources leading to overproduction, leading to excessive inventories, which create unnecessary costs in personnel costs, depreciation costs, and interest costs. The TPS curbs those superfluous costs by making a system that produces at the same rate at which a product can be sold and responds quickly and flexibly to fluctuations in demand. Monden (2006) maintains that this is achieved by Just-In-Time (JIT) production, managed through its *Kanban* System. Implementing a *Kanban* System requires *heijunka* (level production), and an equalized volume of parts taken in to the final assembly line during given time periods. To level production, lead-times must be shortened so that a variety of different parts can be produced quickly each day. Reduced production lead-time is achieved either by small-lot production through reduced set-up time, or by one-piece-at-a-time production by workers who handle multiple processes on the production line. Another pillar of JIT production is *jidoka* (autonomation) or manufacturing 100% non-defective products via a system that automatically manages malfunctions and abnormalities. Additionally, *kaizen* (improvement) activities carried out in all production processes are the driving forces boosting workplace morale on the production line, preventing recurrent malfunctions and abnormalities, and helping to fine-tune standardized work to increase productivity.

Monden (2006) points out that because the TPS uses these unique methods to improve productivity in order to profit even in periods of low economic growth, it constitutes the next revolutionary production system after Taylor's scientific management and Ford's mass production. He also tells us that the TPS has gained a lot of attention in Japan in the era of low growth following the 1973 "oil shock" for its profitability by eliminating waste and cutting costs and has subsequently been adopted by many companies.

Given the above, we can claim that the TPS has strengthened the international competitiveness of a wide range of Japanese manufacturing industries through productivity improvement, greatly contributing to Japan's economic development.

3. The Rise of Strategic Management Theory

We next review the rise of strategic management theory, one of the factors that prompted a new take on the goals of the TPS.

In the wake of the Second Industrial Revolution at the beginning of the 20 century, the concept of business management became a part of the social system. This concept was later developed into a variety of management theories, particularly in the West, and is now one of the fundamental concepts of corporate activity.

There are many ways to look at the major changes in Western management theory over time, but we approach them from six major viewpoints, roughly in order of their origin/rise in popularity: (1) efficiency, (2) organization, (3) humanity, (4) quality, (5) marketing, and (6) business strategy.

From the efficiency viewpoint, the main management theories have been Taylor's (1911) scientific management, Ford's (1922) mass-production system, and Weber's (1947) bureaucratic system. Taylor (1911) influenced broad productivity improvements through task optimization based on time and motion studies. Ford (1922) successfully made the world's first economic car by conceiving and introducing a mass-production system based on simplification, standardization, and specialization of human labor and mechanization of the assembly line. Weber (1947) conceived of bureaucracy as the ultimate organizational function of the industrialized capitalist system. These three men all prioritized attaining efficiency in their thinking about management.

From the organizational viewpoint, the notable management theory is Sloan's (1964) multi-divisional structure with three major contributions: building a decision-making process on management information and knowledge, creating a new model of organizational function that married decentralization with coordinated control over the whole corporation, and inventing divisional management accounting. Sloan's creation of a multi-divisional structure inspired a decentralization trend among large Western corporations at the time as a means of promoting growth by expanding and diversifying businesses.

Third, from the viewpoint of humanity, we have Mayo's (1933) human relations approach, Barnard's (1938) organizational theory, and the motivational theories of Maslow (1965), Herzberg (1959), and McGregor (1960). Through his work on the Hawthorne studies, Mayo (1933) discovered the existence and significance of workers' informal organizational relationships and social motivations. Barnard (1938) held that an individual can develop within collective cooperation and pointed out the importance of communication within an organization. Maslow (1965), Herzberg (1959), and McGregor (1960) provided a framework for a rational theory of motivation through the hierarchy of needs theory, the motivation-hygiene theory, and Theories X and Y, respectively.

The main management theory examples from the quality viewpoint are Shewhart's (1931) quality control (QC), Deming's (1982) total quality control (TQC), and the United States's Malcolm Baldrige National Quality Award (MBNQA). This viewpoint involves the workmanship of commodities new to the early 20th century market. Shewhart (1931) conceived of a statistical QC method to produce good commodities in an efficient and stable manner by controlling factors that increase variation in different parts of the production process and adversely affect quality. Deming (1982) built on his experience practicing QC coaching in Japan after World War II to develop a theory of TQC at the company level. Based on Shewhart and Deming's achievements, the United States government deemed strengthening its industrial competitiveness through improvements in quality and productivity a crucial national strategy, and instituted the MBNQA in 1987. The MBNQA was designed to evaluate overall business quality using criteria such as strategic planning, customer focus and satisfaction, process management, and leadership, and to honor organizations for excellence. This award was one starting point for the rise of the concepts of customer value and customer satisfaction, which would go on to deeply penetrate the world of business management.

We next have the marketing viewpoint, whose principal management theories are Howard (1957), McCarthy (1960), and Kotler's (1967) marketing management theories and Levitt's (1960) marketing myopia theory. Amid the consumption-led economic growth that occurred after World War II, Howard (1957) argued that marketing was its own field of business administration which dealt with a wide range of sales-related issues. McCarthy (1960) and Kotler (1967) proposed fundamentals of marketing management intended to win customers while adapting to environmental changes. Levitt (1960) called on businesses to focus on the value customers gain from their products when defining their company missions. The advent of these marketing theories is arguably one of the triggers that extended the established inside-the-organization management thinking to incorporate the customer, who exists outside of the company.

Lastly, we have the business strategy viewpoint. The principal management theories from this viewpoint are Drucker's (1954) theory of customer creation, Chandler (1962) and Ansoff's (1965) theories of strategic planning, and Porter's (1980, 1985) competitive strategies. While systematically explaining his principles of business management, Drucker (1954) asserted that the only effective purpose of a business is to create a customer. Chandler (1962) said that a company's business strategy development dictates its optimal business structure. In the period of high economic growth following World War II, Ansoff (1965) devised a strategic planning model for strategic corporate decision making founded in research and analysis of products and markets. Porter (1980, 1985) held that strategies to counter the competition to expand market share are even more important in a slow economy, and that positioning in a competitive market determines effective strategy. He thus proposed key strategic concepts such as his Three Generic Strategies of cost leadership, differentiation, and focus; the Five Competitive Forces Shaping the Industry; and cluster analysis. The advent and rise of these strategic management theories focused management thinking on the customer.

The above is an overview of the major changes in Western management theories leading up to the rise of strategic management theory. Over the course of these changes, the key perspectives have undergone a shift from those involving the internal viewpoints of (1) efficiency, (2) organization, (3) humanity, and (4) quality (of goods) to those involving the world outside the company, especially customer orientation, such as (4) quality (of management), (5) marketing, and (6) business strategy.

A number of changes in the business environment led to this shift in perspectives. Essentially, while on the company-side, advancements in manufacturing and production technologies made it possible to supply sophisticated and low-cost goods in large quantities, on the customer side, wealth bolsters a diversification of values and lifestyles. This changed the business environment significantly, where intensifying competition between businesses was accompanied by increasing customer predominance in the market. Amidst these shifts in the business environment perhaps best regarded as social and economic maturation, the key perspectives of management theory greatly changed direction, and the goals of the TPS are in the process of changing with them.

With this awareness in mind, we now turn to three perspectives to consider TPS applications in customer-oriented, cross-sectional BPM.

4. Historical Change and Evolution of the TPS

As the first perspective from which one can examine the use of the TPS for BPM, we describe the historical arc of the changes to and evolution of the TPS.

Figure 1 shows how the main techniques and subsystems that make up the TPS were created and developed along a timeline in accordance with its two pillars, JIT and *jidoka*.

Year	1950	1960	1970	1980	1990	2000
JIT	Pull System	Kanban System			e-Kanban System	
	Fill-Up System of Production		Set-Up Time Reduction			
		Continuous Flow Production				
	Elimination of Intermediate Warehouses					
		Synchronization Among Processes				
	Heijunka					
	Production Sequence Table					
		Truck Transfer System		Logistics Lead Time Reduction		
			Mixed-Load Conveyance			
		10-Day Order System				
			Daily Order System	"Customer-In" System		
Jidoka	Andon	Pokayoke	Fixed-Position Stop System			
			Building Quality In-Process			
	Visual Control Full-Work Control					
	Standardized Work	Autonomated Engine Line				
			Autonomated Lines with NC Machines and Robots			
	Multi-Machine Handling					
	Multi-Process Handling					

Fig. 1.   Changes in the TPS (Created with Data from Toyota Motor Corporation (2012))

From the late 1940s to early 1950s, the pull system (in which one process goes to the preceding process to "pull" the parts it needs, when it needs them, in the exact needed amount) and the fill-up system (in which a preceding process then produces only enough to replace the parts withdrawn by a following process and maintain a minimum inventory of completed parts) were adopted. Along with this initiative, Toyota worked to reduce inventory by eliminating intermediate warehouses that held product between the machining process or stamping process and assembly. The company began to implement other techniques at this time, such as *Andon* to indicate where abnormalities have occurred; other visual controls that prompt managers/supervisors to make quick judgments and take steps to cope with problems; the establishment of standardized work through Takt-Time, working sequence, and standard in-process stock; and assigning multiple machines to one operator. In the late 1950s, as synchronization among production processes advanced, production sequence tables were adopted, which showed the sequence to produce different models based on the mix of models to manufacture in a leveled production plan. In the early 1960s, the *Kanban* System was introduced in all Toyota plants and suppliers, and continuous flow processing that did not go through warehouses began, as did multi-process handling by workers. Techniques such as *pokayoke* and full-work control were also adopted at this time to prevent product defects and machinery malfunctions. The early 1970s saw a reduction in stamping set-up time at all Toyota plants. This record would further improve as JIT quickly advanced in the late 1990s with the adoption of the e-*Kanban* System. The company adopted a fixed-position stop system in the assembly process in the early 1970s and strengthened the system of building quality in-process in the late 1980s to dramatically advance *jidoka*. The autonomated engine line completed in the late 1960s was developed into the automated facilities with NC machines and robots for machining and body processes that arrived in the early 1980s. All of these things were innovations or developments geared toward productivity improvements in the realm of production.

In the early 1960s, the TPS progressed from the production realm to the neighboring realm of logistics. The company adopted a truck transfer system to transport things between plants that separated the loading and unloading tasks from the driving task, so that a driver could switch to another truck that was already loaded when arriving and depart with it right away. This system greatly improved logistics efficiency. In the late 1970s, a circling system of mixed-load conveyance between part plants was adopted, reducing inventory at both parts and assembly plants. The late 1980s saw the elimination of redundant processes and inspections as well as the synchronization of production and logistics processes, reducing logistics lead time. These were innovations or developments geared toward productivity improvement in the realm of logistics.

A still greater transformation than the invention and development of these production and logistics techniques occurred when the company extended the TPS into the order delivery realm, which includes customer contact.

In the late 1960s, the cycle between orders from the dealers and Toyota's production plans changed from a monthly order plan to a 10-day order plan (three cycles per month). In the late 1970s, the company adopted a system to establish a day-by-day sequence of the particulars of a given 10-day order plan. In the early 1990s, the TPS built on these things to construct a "Customer-In" System as one of its sub-systems, which enabled information processing for the whole order delivery process (dealer places a 10-day order with Toyota→customer places a purchase request at the dealer→Toyota produces the vehicle→Toyota dispatches the vehicle to the dealer→the dealer delivers the vehicle to the customer) to take place online and in real time on a high-speed digital line. This greatly reduced the total lead-time between receipt of customer orders to vehicle delivery to the customer and improved the precision of production plans. In other words, in the "Customer-In" System sends the general information about 10-day orders from the dealers to Toyota, while the dealership is simultaneously taking orders from customers on the sales floor. When the concrete details of a customer order are established, such as vehicle model, version, specifications, and factory-installed options, this information is once again put into the same system, and the system immediately outputs the delivery information, allowing the dealers to answer customer questions about the delivery timeline on the spot. From that point up until just before vehicle production begins at Toyota, the same system can be used right from the dealer's sales floor to change the details of the customer's vehicle order (order information) any time the customer wants.

The extension of the TPS into the realm of order delivery is significant. As mentioned above, amidst the intensifying competition between businesses and increasing customer predominance of the market, drastic shifts in the business environment occurred that represent social and economic maturation, the dominance of strategic management theory, and the shift in major management theory viewpoints from an internal to an external focus, particularly with regard to customer orientation. The goals of the TPS changed in tandem. The system was first created to improve productivity at a time when customer orientation was not on managers' minds. The TPS is still used today as it transitions to a customer-oriented system, and what's more, it has gained the "Customer-In" System sub-process to make that customer orientation a reality.

In the context of the TPS's historical changes, its expansion into the order delivery realm, in other words, its goal shift and its construction of the "Customer-In" System, is an evolution of the TPS itself. We will invoke Merton's (1949) manifest and latent function analytics and Fujimoto's (1997) theory of the evolution of social systems to consider this point.

Merton (1949), a sociologist, draws a sharp distinction between the subjective intents and motives of people participating in an action and the objective consequences of that action. The functions that are the objective result of an action, regardless of whether that action has preserved or helped a system prosper, can be divided into manifest functions, which were intended, and latent functions, which were not intended. By this logic, the manifest function of the TPS is to preserve and develop production systems through productivity improvement. However, if we take the three TPS fundamentals that support productivity improvement, i.e., small-lot production of a wide variety of products, *jidoka*, and JIT, and look at them from the customer's standpoint, small-lot production makes it possible to fulfill diverse customer demands by developing a variety of products; *jidoka* enables a company to provide the customer with high-quality, defect-free products; and JIT makes it possible to provide customers with their products with minimal lead-time. We can thus say that the TPS contributes to customer-oriented management strategy as a latent function. We can also consider this latent function of the TPS to be steadily turning into a manifest function as the aforementioned changes in the business environment, the popularity of strategic management theory, and the shift from productivity improvement to customer focus all continue.

Fujimoto (1997) points out that in contrast to biological evolution, which allows for only random mutations (such as miscopied DNA), social system evolution allows for all sorts of system variations to occur as emergent processes, such as rational preemptive actions, choices forced upon us by our environments, coincidences, and unexpected events. Furthermore, these mutated systems will be preserved by organizational routines, program saves, intra-organizational propagation, and inter-organizational propagation. This view of things, too, allows us to recognize the TPS's expansion into the order delivery realm in response to the changing business environment (and in particular the creation and subsequent use of its "Customer-In" System) as an evolution of the TPS as a social system.

5. Customer Orientation in the TPS

For our second perspective on the TPS for BPM, we examine how the TPS, in particular, its sub-system of "Customer-In", increases adaptability to customer needs.

As mentioned previously, the three fundamentals of the TPS are diversified small-lot production, *jidoka*, and JIT. As Ohno (1978) points out, in the early days of the TPS, the small-lot production of a wide variety of products was introduced as a way to improve productivity and compete against the Western system of automobile mass-production within the constraints of Japan's small-scale automotive market. In contrast to this passive response to market constraints, the TPS, with its different goals uses diversified product development based on a business strategy viewpoint to actively and strategically meet diverse customer demands. For example, Toyota combines two strategies: the Toyota brand adopting the cost leadership strategy and the Lexus brand adopting the differentiation strategy, to deploy approximately 100 models in over 170 countries/regions worldwide to create customers, and it receives over 10 million customer vehicle orders per year. Moreover, in order to meet customer demand, each model has a variety of versions, specifications, and factory-installed options, dramatically expanding the possible combinations. To reliably provide high-quality versions of these varied products to customers via *jidoka* manufacturing of 100% non-defective products, it is vital to have a means to link customer order details with Toyota's production plans quickly, exhaustively, and flexibly. Essentially the "Customer-In" System is a subsystem of the TPS built to achieve this aim.

An even greater symbol of the "Customer-In" System's customer focus than its role as a foundation for diversified product development and provision of high-quality products to the customer is its contribution to shortening the total lead time between customer order and final delivery. As Monden (2006) said, JIT production introduced at the beginning of the TPS as a technique to improve productivity contributed toward reduced production lead time. Now, the TPS with its changed goals has expanded from the realm of production and logistics to the realm of order delivery, shifting the focus of lead time reduction from production to the total lead time from order receipt to vehicle delivery. Figure 2 shows the

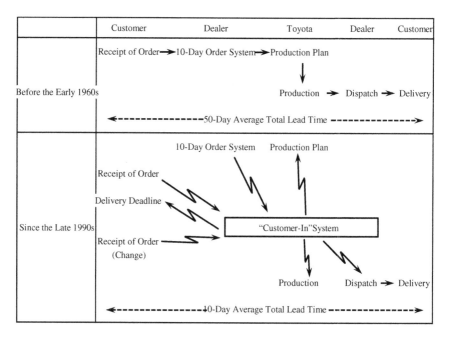

Fig. 2.   Changes in total lead time (Created with Data from Toyota Motor Corporation (2012))

change in total lead time between the early 1960s and the late 1990s when the "Customer-In" System was established. As discussed, under the "Customer-In" System, from the time they submit an order up until just before production begins at Toyota, customers can change their order information at any time. This greatly reduces the total lead time, allowing customers to receive products quickly.

6. Possibilities for the TPS's Further Evolution

As our third perspective for considering the TPS for BPM, we now apply the viewpoints of the pursuit of manufacturability in the technical development stage, environment, and accounting to look at the prospects for further evolution in the TPS.

Firms have recently tended to shift their efforts to improve productivity from manufacturing processes during the mass-production stage to product development processes during the technical development stage. We generally call this the pursuit of manufacturability.

According to Fujimoto (1997), product manufacturing is the repeated transmission of the product design information created during product development from workers or equipment to raw materials or intermediate products during production processes. Labor productivity and equipment productivity are defined as the efficiency of this transmission. For example, the "hours actually worked" for a given worker during a production process comprised value-adding work time, during which design information is actually being transmitted, and incidental time such as walking or waiting, when design information is not being transmitted. Thus, labor productivity increases when either the necessary value-adding work time is shortened, or the percentage of value-adding work time within "hours actually worked" increases.

Pursuing manufacturability is a productivity improvement activity in the early stages of technical development where the product structure (design information) and production process layout are created together during product development either to shorten the value-adding work time in the mass-production stage or to increase the percentage of value-adding work time. This pursuit of manufacturability could potentially bring further evolution to the TPS by expanding its domains of application from production, logistics, and order delivery to product development, thereby achieving even greater reduction in production lead time and thus total lead time.

Meanwhile, in the realm of managerial accounting, environmental management accounting has recently emerged due to an upsurge of environmental awareness in business management. In particular, the use of Material Flow Cost Accounting (MFCA), which looks at production and logistics processes, is growing. According to Nakajima and Kokubu (2008), MFCA quantifies, traces, measures, and manages the flows and stocks of any and all materials within a company's production and logistics processes from input to output in both physical and monetary units. It regards both the desired products and wastes of said processes as types of "products", and, as a rule, calculates accurate costs under the exact same accounting conditions, based on material balance. In the sense that it recognizes the waste management costs overlooked in conventional cost accounting as independent environmental costs, we could call MFCA an elaboration of the traditional type of cost accounting.

MFCA and efficient TPS are both techniques capable of making positive environmental contributions. However, MFCA as an environmental management accounting practice has a limitation: because its calculations do not incorporate time, it cannot directly contribute to JIT's reductions in production or logistics lead time. The new managerial accounting concept invented to overcome this limitation is Imai's "Material Flow Time Cost" (MFTC) (2013). MFTC treats the materials (material inputs) in production and logistics processes as a form of capital and measures the costs of the production/logistics lead time materials required to move through the flow as capital costs.

By making MFTC a part of cost calculations, MFCA becomes a managerial accounting method that can directly contribute to the TPS's reduction of production/logistics lead time through JIT. Thus, integrating the TPS and MFCA into production/logistics processes can further accelerate environmental conservation activities and reduce production/logistics lead time, and total lead time by extension. It is fair to say that this is another possibility for the TPS's future evolution.

7. Conclusion

According to Toyota Motor Corporation (2012), Toyota's business has rapidly globalized since the late 1990s, and the number of employees outside Japan has skyrocketed. This presents the management problem of how to make sure its employees across the globe share the same management values. In response, in April of 2001, Toyota compiled "The Toyota Way 2001", which packaged Toyota's management beliefs and values that were previously passed down as tacit knowledge visibly with the TPS as a base so that they can be understood systematically. In "The Toyota Way 2001", Fujio Chou, who spearheaded the publication and was President of Toyota Motors at the time, called on all of Toyota's global employees to continually ask themselves whether their current way of working was in line with the Toyota Way. Because this version of Toyota Way was not something intended to remain fixed, but rather something that the company should ensure evolves in response to changing times and environments, the year of its formulation, 2001, was appended to its official title. Toyota sought active discussion among its employees about the shape the TPS-based Toyota Way should take in the future.

In light of this, this paper traced the arc of the TPS's historical change and evolution and sought to reveal the changes in the business environment that lie behind it as well as the resulting directional shift in management theory perspectives. One of the conclusions this implies is that the goal of the mature TPS is to shift from its initial goal of productivity improvement within the manufacturing process to focus more on customer-oriented, cross-sectional BPM to increase adaptability to customer needs by offering diversified, high-quality products with minimal lead time. That is the new face of today's TPS.

This paper also subsumed four new points into its management theory. First, it offered a unified view of the relationship between the TPS and the history of management theory; second, it indicated the evolutionary elements in TPS history; third, it reevaluated and reconstructed the basic attributes of the TPS from a customer-oriented perspective; and fourth, it examined the "Customer-In" System that symbolizes the use of the TPS for BPM.

Twenty-first century societies and economies are sure to mature even more, further enhancing the intensification of competition and customer predominance. As this happens, the significance of BPM for customer orientation as well as the significance of the TPS for BPM as demonstrated in this paper will grow more widely acknowledged in both theory and practice.

References

Ansoff, H. I. (1965). *Corporate Strategy*, New York, NY: McGraw Hill.

Barnard, C. I. (1938). *The Functions of the Executive*, Cambridge, MA: Harvard University Press.

Chandler, A. D. (1962). *Strategy and Structure: Chapters in the History of the Industrial Enterprise*, Cambridge, MA: MIT Press.

Deming, W. E. (1982). *Out of the Crisis*, Cambridge, MA: MIT Press.

Drucker, P. F. (1954). *The Practice of Management*, New York, NY: Harper & Row.

Ford, H. (1922). *My Life and Work*, Garden City, NY: Garden City Publishing.

Fujimoto, T. (1997). *Evolution Manufacturing System at Toyota*, Tokyo: Yuhikaku (in Japanese).

Herzberg, F. (1959). *The Motivation to Work*, Hoboken, NJ: John Wiley & Sons.

Howard, J. A. (1957). *Marketing Management: Analysis and Decision*, Homewood, IL: Richard D. Irwin.

Imai, N. (2013). Proposal of the Concept of Material Flow Time Cost: A Study on Possibility of Integrated Evolution of Toyota Production System and Material Flow Cost Accounting, *Journal of Japan Management Diagnosis Association*, Vol. 12, pp. 138–144 (in Japanese).

Kotler, P. (1967). *Marketing Management: Analysis, Planning, Implementation and Control*, Upper Saddle River, NJ: Prentice-Hall.

Levitt, T. (1960). Marketing Myopia, *Harvard Business Review*, pp. 45–56.

Maslow, A. H. (1965). *Eupsychian Management*, Homewood, IL: Richard D. Irwin.

Maxcy, G. & Silberston, A. (1959). *The Motor Industry*, London: George Allen & Unwin.

Mayo, E. (1933). *The Human Problems of an Industrial Civilization*, New York, NY: Macmillan.

McCarthy, E. J. (1960). *Basic Marketing: A Managerial Approach*, Homewood, IL: Richard D. Irwin.

McGregor, D. (1960). *The Human Side of Enterprise*, New York, NY: McGraw Hill.

Merton, R. K. (1949). *Social Theory and Social Structure: Toward the Codification of Theory and Research*, New York, NY: Free Press.

Monden, Y. (2006). *Toyota Production System: Its Theory and System*, Tokyo: Diamond, Inc., (in Japanese).

Nakajima, M. & Kokubu, K. (2008). *Material Flow Cost Accounting: An Innovative Approach of Environmental Management Accounting*, Tokyo: *Nihon Keizai Shinbun Shuppansha* (in Japanese).

Ohno, T. (1978). *Toyota Production System: Beyond Large-Scale Production*, Tokyo: Diamond, Inc., (in Japanese).

Porter, M. E. (1980). *Competitive Strategy: Techniques for Analyzing Industries and Competitors*, New York, NY: Free Press.

Porter, M. E. (1985). *The Competitive Advantage: Creating and Sustaining Superior Performance*, New York, NY: Free Press.

Shewhart, W. A. (1931). *Economic Control of Quality of Manufactured Product*, New York, NY: D. Van Nostrand.

Sloan, A. P. (1964). *My Years with General Motors*, Garden City, NY: Doubleday.

Taylor, F. W. (1911). *The Principles of Scientific Management*, New York, NY: Harper & Brothers.

Toyota Motor Corporation. (2012). History of Toyota, (in Japanese). http://www.toyota.co.jp/jpn/company/history/75years/ (accessed on January 24, 2016).

Weber, M. (1947). *The Theory of Social and Economic Organization*, Oxford: Oxford University Press.

PART II

Case Studies of BPM in Japanese and Korean Companies

Quality-Focused Cost Management by Projects: A Lesson from a Japanese Design and Construction Firm

Masanobu Kosuga

Professor, School of Business Administration,
Kwansei Gakuin University

1. Introduction

Business Process Management (BPM) refers to the control and management of transactions between organizations both within and outside companies by viewing the transaction flows as processes, which is enabled by breaking up the traditional hard/high walls between several organizational units, sharing information and resources among them, and combining their transactions (Lee *et al.*, 2010, preface). BPM is a kind of strategic management system based on visualizing several transaction flows as business processes.

The purposes of this paper are to sum up the main points of research results of the case study on the cost management practices in Company A (name withheld by request). This case explores the implications of *Quality-focused Cost Management* practices by projects from the view point of BPM. It illustrates the roles for cost information in a Japanese construction firm. Furthermore, it shows how a Japanese family business behaves in order to stimulate process improvement and make several strategic decisions.

This paper is an integral part of a series on management systems and management accounting practices in Japanese construction industry (for more details, see Miyamoto, 2004a, 2004b, 2005a, 2005b, 2009, 2010a, 2010b, 2010c, 2011). The research was carried out during 2012–2016. The Head Office at Osaka and Tokyo Main Office were selected as main objects for a case study in this research. Based on the several publications on Company A, this study employed the semi-structured interview method. Interviewees were the senior directors in the Head Office at Osaka, operating officers and several functional managers at Tokyo Main Office. The following is mainly based on the descriptions in its *Corporate Reports* published by Company A during the fiscal years 2012–2016 in order to exclude several possible personal bias and/ or misunderstandings.

2. Overview of Company A

2.1. *Fundamentals of its management philosophy*

In *Corporate Report 2016*, the history of Company A is explained as follows (for more details, see *Corporate Report 2016*, p. 7).

Since its foundation in 1610, the Company, as an architectural specialist, has handled many buildings that have become landmarks, thus playing a vital role in the development of our society. The founder, who was a master builder of shrines and temples, established a business in Nagoya in order to engage in Japanese shrine and temple construction. In the Company, architectural works had to look at vessels to protect life and property, and at the same time, they are considered to be social assets. Architectural works are the culture of their times that is passed on to future generations — Having the pride inherent in such work, all members of the Company refer to the buildings they are involved with as "works of art" with a spirit that has been passed down from the founder. This philosophy is a way of thinking that puts customer dreams first and maintains high-level technology as an architectural specialist (see *Corporate Report 2016*, p. 7).

On the fundamental philosophy of the Company, the Chairman/CEO of the Company gives an explanation as follows:

"Since the founding of our business, we have consistently provided architectural structures that respond to the expectations of our customers based on our management philosophy; that is 'Contribute to society by passing on the best works to future generations'. ...We wishes to maintain a sensitivity to change at all times. To this end, we will continue our ongoing dialog with people everywhere and our diligent efforts to improve our technologies with the aim of providing optimal solutions to the needs of the era. By leveraging the strengths of our whole corporate group, we will contribute to urban creation by building cities and towns where people can live in safety and security, and to achieving a sustainable society with the aim of establishing a path to a better future for the earth" (see *Corporate Report 2016*, p. 3).

2.2. Profiles of the company

Japan has a long tradition of long-lived family businesses. Until recently, Japan was home to the oldest-known family enterprise in the world, a construction company which closed in 2006 after more than 1,400 years of existence (Goydke, 2016, p. 48).

Fig. 1 shows the profiles of the Company. This Company is not a listed company. In other words, it remains a large family enterprise, which

Head Office	Osaka, Japan
Capital	¥50 billion (as of March 31, 2016)
Sales	¥1,284 billion (consolidated, fiscal 2015)
Employees	7,195 (as of January, 2016)
Main Businesses	(a) Undertaking design and supervision of architectural and civil engineering works.
	(b) Studies, research, surveys, planning, evaluation, diagnosis and other engineering and management services for construction, energy supply, regional and urban development, ocean development, space development, environmental preservation, and other projects.
	(c) Land preparation and housing construction.
	(d) Sales and purchasing, leasing, transaction mediation, maintenance, management and appraisal of real estate, as well as real estate investment management.

Fig. 1.   Overview of the company

was funded by a family. There is no division between ownership and management. A family has control over the whole group companies.

Mr. Terunobu Fujimori, Japanese architectural historian, explained the features of the Japanese construction industry as follows (for details, see Setagaya Art Museum, 2016, p. 29).

Industry insiders often speak of the "Big Five" companies (they are *Shimizu, Kajima, Obayashi, Taisei*, and Company A). Japan is the only one country to have so many as five construction companies of this size, each of them housing their own technical research institutes and cultural affairs departments. The traditional master builders ...they built the buildings that they had designed by themselves. This is completely different from the foreign companies, separating design from construction. Design was to be handled by architects, while the buildings were to be constructed by builders.

In Japan, family businesses are called *Dozoku Gaisha* (family firm) or *Daidai Kagyo* (family-like business/multi-generation business), but the terms *Kazoku Keiei* (family management) or *Dozoku Keiei no Kigyo* (family-led enterprise) are also frequently used (Goydke, 2016, p. 49). Company A is a typical enterprise of Japanese family business.

2.3. *Group growth strategy toward 2025*

The Company seeks to provide the best solutions to its customers' business challenges on a global scale to contribute to the realization of a sustainable society through the concerted efforts of its entire group. The President/COO of Company A said, "The Company has taken on the important mission of resolving wide-ranging issues facing society at home and overseas, and of achieving a sustainable society in which people can lead prosperous, happy lives with peace of mind. For that purpose we treat group-wide areas of business as 'cities', and we will contribute to the entire life cycle of these 'cities' from planning and design to construction, maintenance and operation. Our goal is to realize a sustainable society by fulfilling the expectations of society and our customers through close collaboration among all our group companies 'throughout every stage of urban creation'" (*Corporate Report 2016*, p. 11).

In order to realize these aims, the Company has a group strategy which consists of four steps toward the group growth by 2025.

(1) The first step (2014–2016): "Ready to Jump" — securing financial stability and preparing to jump.
(2) The second step (2017–2019): "Group Power" — using its comprehensive group power to add value to society.
(3) The third step (2020–2022): "Challenge" — challenging new fields and achieving results.
(4) The fourth step (2023–2025): "Best Partner" — best partner for society and customers.

2.4. *Financial performance of the company*

Fig. 2-4 show the transition in financial performance of the Company from the fiscal year 2013 to 2015, just in Step 1 plan of its growth strategy.

In *Corporate Report 2016*, review of the past year's activities and preview of activities planned for 2016, the final year of the Step 1 plan, are shown and explained as follows (for details, see *Corporate Report 2016*, p. 12).

"Fiscal 2016 marks the final year of the three-year plan (STEP 1) we launched in 2014 as a basis for improving our earning capabilities to

(Millions of yen)

Fiscal year	2013	2014	2015
Orders received	1,214,335	1,418,103	1,295,029
Revenues	1,020,956	1,150,663	1,284,362
Operating income	11,525	27,741	59,883
Operating margin (%)	1.1	2.4	4.7
Ordinary income	21,709	38,367	68,666
Net income	7,162	23,545	44,140
Net assets	438,468	471,436	521,011
Total assets	1,105,029	1,240,256	1,342,971

Fig. 2.   Income statement and balance sheet (consolidated)

			(Millions of yen)
Fiscal year	**2013**	**2014**	**2015**
Construction business	939,100	1,063,666	1,188,308
Development business	45,929	48,287	46,743
Others	35,926	38,709	49,309

Fig. 3.   Revenues by business (consolidated)

			(Millions of yen)
Fiscal year	**2013**	**2014**	**2015**
Japan	872,155	960,443	1,090,954
Asia	90,399	129,903	134,923
Europe	25,260	33,308	27,783
North America	23,289	25,921	30,701
Others	9,851	1,086	—

Fig. 4.   Revenues by regions (consolidated)

ensure stable management and establishing a foundation for the future growth of our business.... In this year, which is the final year of the STEP 1 plan, we will continue to prioritize efforts to prevent disasters and improve quality at our construction sites in pursuing further improvements in productivity, we will promote group-wide collaboration and partnerships with subcontractors. Moreover, as one of our top priorities, we will work to establish a production system that appropriately meets the needs of society and our customers. We will thereby ensure stable management and strengthen our business foundation to assure the achievement of dramatic advances over the next three years".

3. Organization of the Company

3.1. *Division systems by geographical areas*

The Company consists of three autonomous divisions by geographical areas: Tokyo, Nagoya, and Osaka. They are set as profit centers (not investment centers). Standard organization of Main Office of each division forms several functional-based departments: general affairs, accounting, personnel, sales and business promotion, facility management, design, estimate, procurement, cost control, construction engineering, mechanical and electrical engineering, safety and environment quality, residential service, and engineering.

Head Office unifies the decisions and activities conducted by each division to realize the group-wide optimization. It has six functions conducted by several departments as follows:

(1) Planning functions:
    (a) Corporate Strategic Planning Department
    (b) Public Relations Department
    (c) CSR Promotion Department
    (d) TQM Promotion Department
    (e) Group ICT Promotion Department
    (f) Subsidiaries & Affiliates Department

(2) Management functions:
    (a) General Affairs Department
    (b) Legal Affairs Department
    (c) Personnel Department
    (d) Finance and Accounting Department

(3) Technological Development functions:
    (a) Technology Department
    (b) Research & Development Department

(4) Marketing functions:
    (a) Marketing Department
    (b) Project Development Department
    (c) PPP/PFI Promotion Department
    (d) Engineering Department
    (e) Facility Management Department
    (f) Smart Communication Department

(5) Design functions:
    (a) Design Department

(6) Construction functions:
     (a) Construction Department
     (b) Procurement Department
     (c) Safety and Environment Department

These departments align along the stream of business processes in the construction industry.

3.2. *Corporate philosophy and policies*

In 1899, the Company was actually established in Kobe, and it was incorporated as a general partnership company in 1909. This was 10 years after the Company began doing business in Kobe, and this marked its transition from a sole proprietorship to a corporate enterprise. The Company had its Head Office in Kobe and a Branch Office in Nagoya.

The Chairman/CEO of the Company said, "Based on the strong intention to carry on the tradition of a master builder, the Company integrates the entire process from design to construction while continuing to place the highest priority on customer service. In order to provide integrated construction services, the Company gathered excellent human resources to work in the area of design and engaged in friendly competition with outstanding architects outside the company, while also learning from some of the leading businessmen of the time" (for details, see Setagaya Art Museum, 2016, p. 16).

The *Group Growth Strategy toward 2025* is formulated, based on the *Corporate Philosophy* and several policies as follows:

(1) *Corporate Philosophy*:
     (a) *Management Policy*: "Contribute to society by passing on the best works to future generations."
     (b) *Company Policy*:
          "Take the path of trust, keep good faith and be steadfast."
          "Be industrious and fulfill your responsibilities."
          "Devote yourself to your work with discipline."
          "Act in harmony with the organization."
          "Pursue prosperity for all of society."

(c) *Total Quality Management (TQM) Policy*: "Earn client satisfaction and society's trust through management that persists in stressing quality and challenging creation of new environments."

(d) *Group CSR Vision*: "The Group will enhance dialog with stakeholders, turn these dreams into reality through urban creation, and connect a sustainable society to the future."

(e) *Corporate Code of Conduct*

(2) *Group-wide Policy*:
 (a) Health and Safety Policy
 (b) Quality Policy
 (c) Environmental Policy
 (d) Procurement Policy
 (e) Personnel Information Protection Policy

(3) *Group Message*: "Dreams into Reality for a Sustainable Future."

The Company, as a consolidated group, has been expanding along with affiliates in new areas such as real estate department, civil engineering, and facility management, while pursuing global expansion as well. The *Group CSR Vision*, which was formulated in 2014, is intended to contribute to the realization of a sustainable future through urban creation, drawing on the collective strengths of the Group in the untiring pursuit of *Quality Management* (for details, see Setagaya Art Museum, 2016, p. 17).

3.3. Tradition as a master builder: quality management emphasis

The Chairman/CEO of the Company said, "The Company has the dual nature of being an architecture specialist and a design-build contractor. Just as master builders during Edo era held overall responsibility for quality, consistency handling a project according to the clients wishes from the drawing board (design) stage through to construction and repairs, the intention of the Company is to fully meet the wishes of our clients and society as a building specialist. This is the master builder approach which the Company boned through generations in shrine and temple carpentry, and this spirit of craftsmanship is still at the heart of the Company today".

Furthermore, he explained the tradition of *Quality Management* as a master builder as follows (see Setagaya Art Museum, 2016, pp. 16–17):

"Ever since its inception in 1610, the Company has taken the fundamental approach of a master builder, and this has continued to define the Company through the traditions of specializing in architecture, pursuing craftsmanship, and maintaining trust as a top priority. Past leaders have left us the following words of wisdom:

- People who engage in the business of architecture must be craftsmen of architecture, not merchants of architecture who merely pursue a profit. In order to go their highest and best work, they must not be bound by conflicting interests, but must transcend such interests.
- Architecture does not disappear after a year or two, but remains as an onduring future in the community. It must be perceived not as a mere commodity, but as part of our nation's wealth and a symbol of our culture.
- Our ideal should be not the biggest, but the best."

4. *Phase Gate Management* for Strategic Cost Management

4.1. *Roles of corporate strategic planning department and engineering department*

The *Corporate Strategic Planning Department* in the Head Office of the Company has a significant role to implement *Quality-focused Cost Management* as a strategic cost management system. In order to functionalize this system, this department formulates the *Group Growth Strategy*, *Branding Strategy*, *CSR Strategy*, and three-year plans (STEP 1-4 plans), based on a kind of frameworks of the Balanced Scorecard (BSC). Indeed, formal three-year plans were set from the point of the view, such as *Financial*, *Stakeholders'*, *Business Process*, and *Learning/Innovation Perspectives*. Sales (Revenues), Orders Received, Operating Income, Operating Margin on Sales (%), Net Income, and CO_2 Emission are the most important key performance indicators (KPI) used in the several strategic plans. Neither any item on the balance sheet nor capital costs are made use of in their strategic plans (for the relationships between BSC and BPM, see Smith, 2007).

A noteworthy phenomenon observed in this case, *Policy Management* (that is, *Hoshin Kanri* in Japanese) is used jointly with BSC. The *Hoshin Kanri* has the overall goal of supporting the implementation of strategic goals developed at top management level. Policy is used to support the organization on key priorities and corporate goals throughout the whole organization and to ensure that objectives are translated into operational goals (for details, see Witcher & Butterworth, 2001). BSC is used as a logical thinking framework, and *Hoshin Kanri* is used as an actual strategic management system.

The *Engineering Department* also has a strong influence on the strategic management system of the Company. The roles of this department are as follows:

(1) Analyze outside/inside environments
(2) Conduct *Strategic Positioning Analysis* by 10 business areas and 25 markets
(3) Formulate *Strategy Maps* by markets
(4) Execute *Competitor Analysis* (comparative investigation into *Shimizu, Kajima, Taisei*, and *Obayashi*).

These two departments cooperate with all functional departments to functionalize *Strategic Cost Management* in the whole processes of the Company.

4.2. TQM: Cross-functional management in the company

TQM is the core and most important strategic theme in the Company. It is a *Cross-functional Management* system. According to Okano (2016), *Cross-functional Management* is a Japanese-style mechanism for promoting factors important to the management of a company, such as quality functions, cost functions, and overseas functions of their cross-sectional coordination with related organizations, and implies horizontal organizational management. On this issue, Okano says, "Historically, it was formed amidst the process of introducing Japanese-style TQC (total quality control). It is antithetical to the 'functional management' of Europe and America, which consists of departments' systems of responsibility and authority" (Okano, 2016, p. 139).

Furthermore, Okano adds as follows: "it is closely linked to the characteristics of Japanese-style quality control, which creates an overlap between the functions of each organization and emphasizes cross-functional activities. There was a loose relationship between business and people, and, by overlapping the work itself and getting all employees to commit themselves, the system induced them to take on responsibility. Cross-functional management was introduced in the early 1980s, around the time when TQC was beginning to take place. At the time, there were strong vertical links in organizations, with hierarchical relationships, for example within the manufacturing division and the sales division, and there were barriers to horizontal relationships, due to sectionalism, so communication was difficult. Cross-functional management such as quality assurance or cost controls, and seeking to supervise and improve these functions by promoting them within each department, in order to deal with problems that are related to the horizontal organization, which cannot be solved by one department within the vertical organization" (Okano, 2016, p. 139).

4.3. *Phase gate management: cost management based on the quality improvement and assurance system*

In the *Corporate Report 2016*, the main point of the customer perspectives of its BSC framework of the Company is explained as follows (see *Corporate Report 2016*, p. 19):

"We create 'safe, secure and attractive architectural works of art', and we build in quality at the design and construction stages based on a quality assurance system, thereby satisfying our customers and earning society's trust. We are committed to maintaining and improving the value as social assets of our customers' buildings by support from both aspects of hardware and software from the initial stages of a project as well as support while holding dialog with customers throughout the life cycles of their buildings."

The Company constructs their quality improvement system and puts it to practical use both for their cost reduction/ensuring profits and quality assurance of a project. They describe this system as follows (for details, see *Corporate Report 2016*, p. 19): The Company incorporates quality in their works during the design and construction stages in accordance with their *Quality Assurance System*, called *Phase Gate Management* system, which provides a set of standardized workflows for the quality assurance process followed in projects based on TQM. Also, the Company implements their cost reduction and cost improvement activities based on this system positively.

Phase Gate in this system means a position where agreement between the customer and the Company is confirmed, and a decision is made on the advisability of advancing to the next phase. *Phase Gate Management* consists of seven stages as follows:

(1) *Phase 0* (Order acquisition activities): the goal of this stage is the receipt of order for basic design to meet several fundamental requirements of customer's project plan. Value proposal through sales activities is most important in this phase. *Life-cycle Costs* on the customer side and total costs of the project are estimated and used for sales activities. At the stage of *Phase 0*, many things are uncertain. As many basic items have not been decided, they are treated as a kind of postulates for estimating costs.

(2) *Phase 1* (Basic plan): In this stage, the Company starts to formulate the basic plan till getting the "design order."

(3) *Phase 2* (Basic design): After getting the "design order", the customer makes up some kind of facility plans. The Company strives to prepare "basic design", starts to (1) formulate a construction plan, (2) estimate the total costs of the project, and (3) make a personnel plan. The goal of this stage is the receipt of "detailed design". Design, Engineering, and Estimate Departments are the main actors in this phase.

(4) *Phase 3* (Detailed design): During this stage, technological assessment is put into operation. This is the most important phase for the quality assurance and improvement process. The end of this phase is "conclusion of contract". At this point, the Company makes a decision on whether to accept the order or not. Several cost reduction activities are examined at all departments in the Company. VE/VA is promoted lead by Engineering Department. Procurement Costs, Design Costs, Construction Costs (mainly, Labor Costs), and others are considered over and over in order to lower the total costs and come up to the acceptable levels.

(5) *Phase 4* (Preparation): After receipt of the order, the Company starts (1) to prepare constructing the project, and (2) to formulate their facilities plans in order to confirm the completion of their preparation.

(6) *Phase 5* (Construction): In this phase, the Company makes intensive efforts on construction supervision/management and pre-delivery examinations. The final end of this phase gate is "completion and delivery". Comprehensive project evaluation is done at this point. These activities are vital factors to assure the quality of the project. The original budgets set by Accounting Department are important cost targets at this stage. All activities in the construction processes are controlled within acceptable amounts approved by budgets.

(7) *Phase 6* (After-sale service): After "completion and delivery", the customer must start Facility Management activities. So, the Company conducts "SC survey" and "post-completion inspection" actively toward the beginning of after-sales service phase in order to seek a new business chance.

In *Corporate Report 2016*, the Company explains the *Phase 6* as follows (see *Corporate Report 2016*, p. 39):

"We also implement further improvements based on customer feedback acquired through such tools as customer satisfaction surveys in an effort to realize diversified expectations and to achieve superior quality".

For the reason stated above, it is clear that *Phase Gate Management* in the Company corresponds to *Quality-focused Cost Management* system by projects. This system has been positioned as activities involving the entire company, and they are carried out by all members. Okano (2016) says, "This is due to the thorough implementation of causal management, which takes the view that quality and costs are built in on site, based on awareness that quality and costs are decided prior to the design stage" (Okano, 2016, p. 140).

5. Conclusion

Company A performs *Phase Gate Management* as a *Quality-focused Cost Management* based on BPM. The organization of the Company is a kind of process-based organization because functional departments line up along the *Phase Gate* system. Phase Gates are set at every business process. Moreover, this company is not a listed company. Therefore, ROI, ROE, Stock Price, Capital Costs, and so on are disregarded in the formal management control system. They seek only satisfactory, acceptable profits in order to continue to exist from now on.

The following deserves our attention: "The Company has always maintained an ethos of actively adopting new technologies and advanced designs with an eye toward the rest of the world. We are not resting on our laurels from a 400-years history in the construction industry, but rather we will continue to fearlessly engage in new endeavors with the support of our clients. This corporate climate of rising to new challenges is an important source of energy for the Company" (see Setagaya Art Museum, 2016, p. 17).

In conclusion, quality and cost management activities in Company A are involving the entire company, and all the members of this organization share the view that (1) quality and costs are built in on-site, (2) quality and costs are decided mainly prior to the design stage, and (3) quality and costs are managed at all *Phase Gate* by all departments.

References

Goydke, T. (2016). Japanese Family Businesses, *Routledge Handbook of Japanese Business and Management*, P. Haghirian, (ed.), London, UK: Routledge, pp. 48–58.

Lee, G., Kosuga, M., Nagasaka, Y. & Sohn, B. (eds.), (2010). *Business Process Management of Japanese and Korean Companies*, Singapore: World Scientific Publishing Co., Pte. Ltd.

Miyamoto, K. (2004a). Framework for Analysis of Worker Performance in the Construction Industry, *Osaka Gakuin Corporate Intelligence Review*, Vol. 3, No. 3, pp. 45–63 (in Japanese).

Miyamoto, K. (2004b). Strategic Cost Management in the Construction Industry, *Osaka Gakuin Corporate Intelligence Review*, Vol. 4, No. 1, pp. 51–62 (in Japanese).

Miyamoto, K. (2005a). Some Issues in Management Accounting: A Case Study of a Japanese Design-Build Constructor Company, *JICPA Journal*, Vol. 17, No. 6, pp. 32–37 (in Japanese).

Miyamoto, K. (2005b). A Study on the Estimate of the Total Cost of the Project in the Construction Industry, *Osaka Gakuin Corporate Intelligence Review*, Vol. 5, No. 2, pp. 33–67 (in Japanese).

Miyamoto, K. (2009). A Study on Knowledge Management in the Construction Industry, *Osaka Gakuin Corporate Intelligence Review*, Vol. 9, No. 1, pp. 55–67 (in Japanese).

Miyamoto, K. (2010a). A Study on Procurement Management in the Construction Industry and its Accounting Information, *Osaka Gakuin Corporate Intelligence Review*, Vol. 9, No. 3, pp. 53–63 (in Japanese).

Miyamoto, K. (2010b). A Study on Supply Chain Management in the Construction Industry, *Osaka Gakuin Corporate Intelligence Review*, Vol. 10, No. 1, pp. 65–92 (in Japanese).

Miyamoto, K. (2010c). Production Planning and Control and the Coordination of Project Supply Chain, *Osaka Gakuin Corporate Intelligence Review*, Vol. 10, No. 2, pp. 69–93 (in Japanese).

Miyamoto, K. (2011). Lean Project Delivery and Supply Chain Management, *Osaka Gakuin Corporate Intelligence Review*, Vol. 11, No. 1, pp. 27–60 (in Japanese).

Nonaka, I. & Takeuchi H. (1995). *The Knowledge Creating Company: How Japanese Companies Create the Dynamics of Innovation*, New York, NY: Oxford University Press.

Okano, H. (2016). Accounting in Japanese Corporations: Cost Designing for Product Development, *Routledge Handbook of Japanese Business and Management*, P. Haghirian, (ed.), London, UK: Routledge, pp. 137–149.

Setagaya Art Museum. (2016). *400 Years of Architectural Challenges*, Tokyo, Japan: Setagaya Art Museum.

Smith, R. F. (2007). *Business Process Management and the Balanced Scorecard: Using Processes as Strategic Drivers*, New Jersey, NJ: John Wiley & Sons, Inc.

Witcher, B. J. & Butterworth R. (2001). Hoshin Kanri: Policy Management in Japanese-owned UK Subsidiaries, *Journal of Management Studies*, Vol. 38, No. 5, pp. 651–674.

Corporate Strategy and Business Process Innovation in Japanese Company: A Case of Panasonic Corporation

Aiko Kageyama
MBA, School of Business Administration, Kwansei Gakuin University
Former Research Fellow, Hiroshima University

Masanobu Kosuga
Professor, School of Business Administration, Kwansei Gakuin University

1. Introduction

In this global society, many of the Japanese corporations are performing their activities based on their own corporate strategies and organization-wide innovations in order to cope with, challenge the rapidly changing and severe environments, and create their corporate value. Business Process Management (BPM) is one of the significant tools for facilitating several innovations which the leading companies have adopted in the world. It has been evolving with impressive leaderships and technologies.

This paper intends to focus on *Panasonic Corporation* (Panasonic) which provides a successful case of current business process innovations based on BPM for decades in Japan. Since fiscal year 2010, Panasonic has aimed to be a *"No.1 Green innovation company in the electronics industry"* to make solutions for the global environmental problems. To achieve this aim, Panasonic has concentrated on making the synergies within the group, has reformed/improved their business processes, and has restructured their whole group companies.

This paper starts from revising the paper of the previous version, that is, Kosuga (2010) and Lee *et al.* (2010) in the following section mainly described about 2000s, and expands the timespan considered to Panasonic's diligent efforts in order to reform their organizations and management systems after the midterm plan: *GP3* in fiscal 2008–2010. The contents and several descriptions in this paper are mainly based on its *Annual Reports*. Needless to say, this paper will not discuss all the changes Panasonic has made. The paper mostly focuses on several business innovations in their midterm plans to build the foundation of finance and several systems for the growth.

At present, Panasonic is working towards the goals for the year 2018, which is the 100th anniversary year of the establishment. One of the goals is to achieve 10 trillion yen of sales (consolidated) in fiscal 2019. Panasonic has remarkably improved its business systems and financial condition, spending on several years of innovations, which were based on the strategies with the eagerness for growth.

2. Business Innovations in Panasonic in the 2000s

2.1. *"Deconstruction" and "Creations": Value Creation 21 Plan*

Value Creation 21 Plan was a midterm plan that started from fiscal 2002 to 2004 with the goal that the company should increase net sales (consolidated) by approximately 1,400 billion yen. The core elements of the plan included the structural reforms with an emphasis on profitability and efficiency improvement and the creation of a new growth strategy. The most important concept of this plan was shifting all focus to "Creation" for a "lean and agile" Panasonic through *Deconstruction* (for details, see Lee *et al.*, 2010).

With this plan, Panasonic challenged to transform into a new corporate model called a *Super Manufacturing Company* which was a firm that retained a commitment to providing truly customer-oriented services and had outstanding strength in components and devices backed by leading-edge technologies and manufacturing products at speed with quick responsiveness to changing market needs.

To be a *Super Manufacturing Company*, Panasonic reclassified its business segments and established four new business segments as AVC Networks (digital broadcasting systems area, mobile communications area, and data storage devices area), home appliances, components and devices (semiconductors area and display devices area), and industrial equipment in order to (1) deal with changing market needs and (2) maximize growth.

2.2. The first trial of business process innovation based on IT innovation: Manufacturing reforms

In order to reform the traditional business system of autonomous divisional management and allocate resources effectively to a whole company, Panasonic established an independent Manufacturing Center which provided their services for various *Product Divisions, Business Groups*, and/or *Business Units*. This center interactively connected and integrated electronic communication networks.

Furthermore, Panasonic introduced the *Cell-style Production System* at various manufacturing locations, while reducing inventory, parts, and material costs and also Supply Chain Management (SCM) was implemented for managing products and factory shipments not on a monthly but on a weekly basis. *Cell-style Production* is a system that single worker carries several manufacturing operations of products and sometimes to the end of processes. This *Cell-style Production* system improved productivity and employees' job satisfaction and resulted in remarkable improvements of cost-competitiveness by conducting continuous improvements, shortening delivery times, and minimizing inventories.

Panasonic has fully utilized IT in order to achieve the aims and reduced lead times in all the processes from R&D and design to parts and materials procurement, manufacturing, and sales.

2.3. The second trial of business process innovation: Restructuring domestic consumer sales and distribution

The second trial, "Restructuring of Domestic Consumer Sales and Distribution" was carried out in fiscal 2001. The aims of these projects were to create a highly efficient structure so as to ensure an agile response to customer needs and to benefit from a cost reduction in the increased market share. In order to implement these reforms, Panasonic reorganized the corporate consumer products sales divisions, sales functions within individual product divisions, and the advertising division into two new divisions: Corporate Marketing Division for "Panasonic Brand" and Corporate Marketing Division for "National Brand". Furthermore, Panasonic consolidated several companies into a single company in several business areas. As a result, these reforms have enabled Panasonic to ensure a more speedy response to changing customer needs.

In order to accelerate to be a *Super Manufacturing Company*, Panasonic implemented group-wide Research and Development and Design *(R&DD)* Reforms. This trial was aimed to create new and competitive products, as well as management initiatives such as IT improvements. In these Panasonic group-wide *R&DD Reforms*, a common platform structure was built by creating *Core Technology Platforms* and *Strategic Product Platforms*. With this new structure, Panasonic became capable of focusing on several resources for the development of strategic products that would be able to contribute to the overall growth of the Group.

2.4. *Group-wide business and organizational restructuring under Value Creation 21 Plan and Leap Ahead 21 Plan*

In January 2003, with eliminating the counterproductive and overlapped businesses, Panasonic reorganized the whole group structure and built 14 *Business Domain Companies*. This trial was aimed to delegate the authorities and responsibilities in order to promote autonomous management and decision making and to facilitate efficient allocation of management resources, which was expected to maximize corporate value of the entire Panasonic Group. This new structure enabled Panasonic to provide the most effective solution services for the customers and make optimum use of group-wide R&D resources.

Panasonic continuously implemented the organizational reform in 2004, whereby the Headquarters would empower each of the *Business Domain Company*. With this new structure, Panasonic revised the performance evaluation measures for *Business Domain Companies*. In this new system, their performances were measured and evaluated based on two result-based measures, Capital Cost Management (CCM) for evaluating capital efficiency and cash flow for evaluating a company's ability to generate cash. Both of these measures were applied to each *Business Domain Company*'s performance on a global consolidated basis.

With *Value Creation 21 Plan* and several reforms for "Deconstruction and Creation", obvious improvement had appeared in its performance and Panasonic moved on to the next midterm plan named *Leap Ahead 21 Plan* from fiscal 2005 to 2007. This plan was implemented to achieve global excellence by 2010 to fulfill its mission of creating value for customers and establish a foundation for sustainable growth in the 21st century. In *Leap Ahead 21 Plan*, the overseas initiative played a vital role of overseas operations as a "Growth Engine" in expanding business and enhancing overall earnings (for details, see Lee *et al.*, 2010).

Under this plan, Panasonic accelerated business and organizational reforms that began in fiscal 2004 and the initiatives of "selection and concentration of businesses" and "closure and/or integration of locations", had been autonomously carried out by each *Business Domain Company*.

2.5. *Management innovation through IT and Corporate Cost Busters Project*

Panasonic had invested heavily in IT infrastructures for 5 years since 2002. The Company had constructed Corporate IT Architecture (CITA) in order to serve as the standard and shared infrastructure for the Panasonic Group. Based on this architecture, Panasonic expedited its manufacturing process, strengthened its speedy response capabilities to rapidly changing business environment, and reduced several costs of information systems. In addition to cost and inventory reductions, CITA has played a significant role by shortening development/production lead times.

In June 2003, Panasonic also launched *Corporate Cost Busters Project* aimed at lowering expenses company-wide with the target achieved by 2005. *Second Corporate Cost Busters Project* began from fiscal 2006 and it also aimed to lower costs in every aspect of management company-wide and challenged to reduce costs by approximately 220 billion yen during the period.

2.6. GP3 Plan to be a manufacturing-oriented company

GP3 Plan had been implemented from fiscal 2008 to 2010 and its name represented *"Global Progress, Global Profit, and Global Panasonic"*. This plan had visions as "double-digit growth in overseas sales accelerating business development in emerging markets", "four strategic businesses (digital AV networks, appliance solutions, car electronics, and black box devices) maximizing group synergies to drive growth" and "continuous 'Selection and Concentration' as concentrating resources on competitive and profitable business areas".

Another goal of *GP3 Plan* was to expand the group-wide innovation activities to transform Panasonic into a *Manufacturing-oriented Company* which combined all business activities toward the launch of products, thereby contributing the creation of customer value. Panasonic also focused on the rigorous pursuit of cost reductions and adopting a company-wide process that sought to rigorously lower costs from the earliest stage of product development.

To achieve the goals of *GP3 Plan*, Panasonic worked to generate double-digit growth in overseas sales, expand strategic businesses, and reinforce the management structure through manufacturing innovation, also accelerating environmental sustainability management. Panasonic focused on strengthening the management structure and reducing fixed costs, but the performance did not grow enough because of the worldwide economic depression in those days.

3. Key Dimensions of Business Innovations in Panasonic

3.1. The first key dimension: Commodification

Through the midterm plans, business process innovations in Panasonic had been implemented along three key dimensions: (1) *Commodification*, (2) *SCM*, and (3) Customer Relationship Management (CRM).

Panasonic had focus on the *Commodification* of original, inimitable, and competitive products and developed what was called "V-products". V-products were made with "black-box technologies" which could not be followed easily by competitors and should be the "universal designed" for anyone to use.

Panasonic also built the platform system for strategic products technologies so that the research group from different domain companies or affiliate companies could join over the production in order to shorten the process cycle time and to provide several products/services which are able to gain customer satisfaction.

Producing V-products was supported by newly established Panasonic Design Company which had one of the representative roles of creation for *Value Creation 21 Plan* (fiscal 2002–2004) whose key phrase was "Deconstruction and Creation".

Panasonic Design Company had the top-down system to create some innovative designs of products. As an independent specialist group, it managed the whole group's design of products, and Panasonic had remarkable achievement and some of the products were even awarded.

From the perspective on the first dimension of business process innovations (that is, *Commodification*), Panasonic should be appraised highly because whole group has made positive efforts to shorten the time to the markets actively.

3.2. The second dimension: SCM

Panasonic had built group-wide management information system called *Global Information System* since 1995 and also introduced SCM to manage the amount of the production and inventories. With SCM, it was expected that Panasonic gained the profitability and efficiencies by sharing information and streamlined the business processes, which was difficult when the organization was vertical and management resources were partially optimized.

Panasonic also began the SCM innovative project to shorten and improve the due date for deliveries for the customer satisfaction which was essential to attain competitive advantage. This SCM dimension is interpreted as a process that consist of procurement, manufacturing, logistics and operating services, and its final goal was to shorten the lead time. To manufacture the V-products in the shortest lead time, the combination of SMC and *Commodification*-enabled production process keep to a schedule for right deliveries due.

3.3. The third dimension: CRM

Panasonic's CRM process consisted of advertisement, marketing, and operating services. Its goal was to enhance the sales by providing quick and flexible customer service including the deliveries in the shortest schedule.

During the period of *Value Creation 21 Plan* (fiscal 2002–2004), Panasonic set up two corporate marketing divisions to strengthen the function of marketing, advertisement, and publicities, the corporate marketing divisions for *Panasonic brand* and for *National brand*. These divisions were allowed to empower to make decision on the sales, implemented strategic investments for advertisement of V-products, and also dealt with the customers' needs carefully and quickly.

For V-products, Panasonic integrated R&DD–manufacturing–sales process and manufactured core parts of the products at their own facilities with their own technologies, which shortened the development time. In addition to them, Panasonic's "new product strategies for 'high-quality/low-price" products were implemented actively so that Panasonic could devote the resources massively.

Panasonic also focused on and did start selling a product simultaneously to the world to expand sales area and gain profitability. For example, Panasonic launched a new plasma TV, *VIERA* into Japan, the US and Europe in May 2005 at one time.

3.4. Continuous organization reform

In addition to these three dimensions: *Commodification, SCM, CRM,* Panasonic had implemented several management challenges as reforming the systems and organizations to delegate the authorities and responsibilities more and more. Panasonic used to run the business under the autonomous divisional management system for a long time. Panasonic called their divisions "company", which were responsible for one product. But this divisional system was abolished in the early 2000s. As already mentioned above, the Domains were built for new systems and/or important function of their manufacturing process became independent and autonomous center or laboratories to provide the technical skills or technologies widely over the Domains, which shorten the development time and/or lead time in production processes.

Panasonic had also challenged to achieving their goals: (1) to gain the expected cash flow and (2) to attain the targeted Return on Equity (ROE). Panasonic improved the original management tool, *CCM* by focusing on their balanced sheet items, especially capital costs. *CCM* aimed to enhance capital efficiency. *CCM* is a kind of residual income, and it was used in order to evaluate the performance of divisional management control.

CCM is calculated as follows:

CCM = (Income before Tax − Interest Earned + Interest Expense − Cost of Asset Invested)

Panasonic originally decided a rate of *CCM* as 8.4% for all the divisions evenly in the early 2000s. *CCM* is also an indicator for evaluating Return on Invested Capital (ROIC). Therefore, when *CCM* is over zero, it was interpreted that the expected minimum returns by the capital market were achieved.

However, this type of the financial indicators may not be efficient enough for BPM and business process innovations. Several non-financial indicators developed on the perspectives: (1) financial, customers, internal business processes, and learning/growth, are more supportive for BPM and innovations. Indeed, Panasonic uses many non-financial indicators positively because they reflect and visualize each of their business processes.

4. Toward the Sustainable Growth for Fiscal 2018

4.1. *Green Transformation 2012 Plan*

GP3 Plan (the midterm plan for fiscal 2008–2010) were taken over to the next plan, *Green Transformation 2012 (GT12) Plan* (fiscal 2011–2013), with the result of less profitability and low growth planned because of the worldwide recession in those days. *GP3 Plan* also left the task that *Commodification* should be more considered and focused, which would be challenged in *GT12 Plan*.

Including that, *GT12 Plan* mainly focused on the global environmental issues and Panasonic decided to start the new themes of the plan: "Paradigm shift for growth," and "Laying a foundation to be a Green Innovation Company".

This paradigm shift for growth had three facets as follows:

(1) shift from existing businesses to new businesses such as energy,
(2) shift from Japan-oriented to globally-oriented,
(3) shift from individual product-oriented to business-oriented solutions and systems.

To evaluate if these paradigm shifts were achieved or not, Panasonic started to use the new performance indicators called *Transformation Indicator*. To be concrete, indicators for type (1) shifts mentioned above were several sales-related ratios for six key businesses and sales of energy systems business, indicators for type (2) shifts were overseas sales ratios and sales of emerging countries, and indicators for type (3) shifts were sales and overseas sales ratios for systems and equipment business.

However, because of the flood in Thailand which affected the global supply chain of Panasonic badly, serious decline in sales, large reductions in sales prices, generous increases in raw material costs and appreciation of the yen, Panasonic had not achieved the goals of *GT12 Plan*.

In 2011, Panasonic reorganized their group structure into the three business areas as consumer, solutions, and components/devices, which consisted of nine *Domain Companies* and one marketing sector. This new structure was built, based on the new business model with the strong customer-conscious perspective so that Panasonic could connect directly and quickly to their customers locally and globally.

Under this structure, the *Domain Companies* combined the products and services across the domains and sold the products of other domains. Also, with the resource from SANYO and other subsidiary companies, Panasonic concentrated more on the environmental- and energy-related businesses.

For the head office reformation, Panasonic separated the business promotion and support function. Panasonic also established the *Professional Business Support Sector* to assist in promoting business operations and carry out corporate functions at the frontline so that the head office concentrated on designing and implementing strategies for the groups and promote the portfolio management for businesses and technologies.

Panasonic emphasized that it should have the customer-based focus with "Eco & Smart solutions", not the product-based focus, which was spread across the four strategic and distinguished spaces, (1) residential space, (2) non-residential space including offices, factories, stores, and hospitals, (3) mobility-encompassing automobiles, and (4) aircraft and personal.

With the goals to be a Green Innovation Company, Panasonic started to make a foundation so as to increase profitability based on growth and to enhance contribution to the environment.

4.2. *Cross-value innovation 2015 Plan*

From fiscal 2014, Panasonic launched the new 3 years midterm plan (fiscal 2014–2016), *Cross-Value Innovation 2015 Plan* (*CV2015 Plan*), challenging four goals, which were (1) to turn around unprofitable business, (2) to expand business and improve efficiency shifting from *In-House Approach*, (3) to improve financial position, and (4) to accomplish the growth strategy from customers' point of view. To start this plan in fiscal 2014, Panasonic reorganized the group structure. The divisional management system was reintroduced. It consisted of four companies: appliances company, eco-solutions company, AVC networks company, and automotive & industrial systems company. Under these companies, there were 49 business divisions to be responsible for R&D, production, and sales globally. Each division was autonomous but followed the strategies each head company planned. All the values and strengths of the group were gathered and crossed from/between each employee, division, company, and the head office. These endeavors generate the significant value for the customers.

In fiscal 2015, the 2nd year of *CV2015 Plan*, Panasonic reorganized the divisions from 49 to 43. To achieve *CV2015 Plan*, each division was expected to gain the operating profit margin on sales by 5%. Panasonic emphasize *Cross-Value Innovation* with synergy between the companies, divisions, technologies, spaces, ideas, workforces, and products. Based on the company's core *"DNA of Consumer electronics"* with the new structure, Panasonic considered to adopt the customer's life style along with business and allocate the resource to the right place.

4.3. Global growth strategy

Panasonic has been challenging to achieve about 10 trillion yen of sales (on consolidated basis) in 2018. For this challenge, Panasonic clearly demonstrated the product areas such as consumer electronics, housing, automotive, B to B solutions and devices, and also segmented the global business map into three regions, Japan, Americas/EU (including central and south America), and "Strategic regions" which includes Asia, China, the Middle East, and Africa.

For the growth in strategic regions, *Strategic Regions Promotion Division* was established in 2014 and the new Executive Vice-president to whom the full authority was delegated was appointed and made to reside in Delhi, India for the local operations with the concept of *"Stop being dependent of Japan"*.

Panasonic has continued concentrating on the strategy for business overseas, especially for the strategic regions. In 2015, Panasonic Appliances Asia Pacific (AP Asia) in Malaysia and Panasonic Appliance China (AP China) were established. These companies adopted self-sustaining management and were delegated much authority and responsible for development, manufacturing, and sales of products based on the local needs.

Panasonic also strategically launched the joint venture with the local company of Israel, TowerJazz for the semiconductor business and purchased a Turkish manufacturer of electrical materials, VIKO Electrik, for Housing business in 2015. The purposes of these decisions were to expand each business, region, and sales for the group's further growth, and these companies were expected to improve efficiency against *In-House Approach*. Subsequently in 2016, Panasonic consolidated a US-based industrial refrigerated and freezer display case manufacturer, Hussman Corporation, which increased the overseas sales in the first quarter of fiscal 2017.

4.4. The improvement for the evaluation of divisional system

Panasonic has been working on enhancing the efficiency of its capital and building a robust financial position to maximize the corporate value. To achieve these purposes mentioned above, the rate of *CCM* was remade to evaluate each business at the division level.

With the new *CCM* rate, Panasonic is able to expect returns over the capital costs for each division, considering the business and region aspects. In the calculation of capital cost, the invested capital was multiplied by the business division rate (expected rate of return by investors) between 4 and 16% which was changed from the single rate of 8.4% for the whole group.

CCM by business division is checked quarterly on the basis of the number of goals achieved. If the goals have not been not achieved enough, then the divisions are requested to make and implement a specific improvement plan. Moreover, *CCM* is used for the investment decision making to examine the potential returns with the risk items, based on *Risk-Return Approach.*

In addition to *CCM* and other performance measures such as cash flow, rate of operating income, and the important Key Performance Indicator (KPI), Panasonic also improved the performance evaluation system to encourage the divisions to face the challenges for further growth actively. The divisions have been evaluated with not only the financial indices but also the non-financial indices as the market share of the business field and the business growth since fiscal 2016. Additionally, *option KPI* was added for the evaluation for each division. For example, the sales overseas was added as a KPI for the evaluation of the housing division where it has been working on enhancing the overseas market.

4.5. The results of the CV2015 Plan

Panasonic achieved the goals of *CV2015 Plan* at the end of fiscal 2015, a year ahead of the schedule. The goals were to obtain (1) 350 billion yen of operating profit with over 5% of the operating profit ratio in each division in fiscal 2016 and (2) 600 billion yen cumulative total in fiscal 2014–2016 of free cash flow. During fiscal 2014–2016, Panasonic had reformed their organizational structures several times in order to make the Panasonic group and their divisions enhance their abilities to increase profit autonomously.

As a result of the continuous reformations of their organizations, Panasonic has also reduced fixed costs and increased the earnings during the midterm plans. However, the earning structure was considered to be shifted into the new structure such that the earnings are increased by sales expansion. For this shift, Panasonic has concentrated on improving the sales and profitability of large business divisions (air-conditioners, lightning, housing systems, automotive systems, rechargeable battery, and Panahome) that have over 300 billion yen of sales but less than 5% of operating profit ratios.

5. Conclusion

Panasonic has emphasized the "Growth" through all activities and decisions within the Panasonic group for a decade. For the future "Growth", Panasonic has focused on the following:

(1) Strong reinforcement of divisions' autonomy for each management. For this, from fiscal 2018, each division will be able to increase/decrease its internal capital by divisions' decision to control the costs of capital. The head-office expects divisions' to be strongly capital-conscious and risk-return-conscious which will lead to the improvement of capital efficiency for the whole group. Also, new evaluation rates for *CCM* were customized for each division after due consideration of the characteristics of businesses and regions so that the divisions are evaluated correctly.

(2) Localization of the business process. Panasonic has accelerated the shifting from *In-House Approach* by means of M&A and alliances in order to be more competitive and to increase the local efficiency and customer value.

(3) Formulation of business areas and regions (see Fig. 1), which are expected to "cross value" of the group.

(4) Cooperation and interaction based on the knowledge, abilities, technologies, and workforces across the companies and divisions in order to achieve the goals and to develop new products by *"crossing-value"*.

Panasonic launched Manufacturing Innovation Toward 2018 (MIT) in fiscal 2016, which is the plan to strengthen 200 major manufacturing facilities in the world where they perform the manufacturing with high productivity based on the keywords: fastest, cheapest, and high-quality.

	Japan	Americas/EU	Strategic Regions
Consumer Electronics			○
Housing	○		○
Automotive	○	○	
BtoB Solutions	○	○	○
Devices			

○: Regions and business areas where a shift in emphasis of management resources is needed.

Fig. 1.　Formulating growth strategies in 5 business areas × 3 Global Regions
[Panasonic Corporation, *Annual Report* 2014, p. 14]

This activity is also associated with the Panasonic Asia-Pacific and Panasonic China so that whole group companies share the same consciousness for manufacturing with continuous innovation and improvement.

References

Kosuga, M. (2009). Business Process Management in Japanese Firm: The Case of Panasonic Corporation, *Journal of Business Administration* (*Shougaku Ronkyu*), Kwansei Gakuin University, Vol. 57, No. 3, pp. 27–59 (in Japanese).

Kosuga, M. (2010). Business Process Innovations in Panasonic Corporation; A Case Study, *Business Process Management of Japanese and Korean Companies*, G. Lee, *et al.*, (eds.), Singapore: World Scientific Publishing Co., Pte. Ltd. pp. 63–77.

Lee, G., Kosuga, M. & Nagasaka, Y. (eds.). (2006). *Strategic Process Management: Theory and Practice*, The Japanese Association of Management Accounting Research Project Series No. 4, Tokyo, Japan: Zeimu-keiri-kyokai (in Japanese).

Lee, G., Kosuga, M., Nagasaka, Y. & Sohn, B. (eds.). (2010). *Business Process Management of Japanese and Korean Companies*, Singapore: World Scientific Publishing Co., Pte. Ltd.

Nihon Keizai Shinbun. (February 19, 2013). Panasonic Introduced the Divisional System for the First Time in Twelve Years, from the Development to Operation as a Whole (electric version in Japanese).

Nihon Keizai Shinbun. (March 11, 2015). Panasonic Let each Division Manage the Capital Cost for the Growth of Medium and Long Terms (electric version in Japanese).

Nihon Keizai Shinbun. (November 2, 2015). Assessors for the Improvement Make Strong Factories of Panasonic (electric version in Japanese).

Nihon Keizai Shinbun. (January 14, 2016). Panasonic Starts New System from Fiscal 2018, the Divisions Increases and Decreases the Capital (electric version in Japanese).

Panasonic Corporation, *Annual Report* (2010–2016).

Panasonic Corporation, Press Release, (April 6, 2015). Starting the 'MIT-2018, the Group-Wide Activity for Building the Strong Base.

Panasonic Corporation, *Quarterly Report filed with the Japanese Government Pursuant to the Financial Instruments and Exchange Law of Japan*, For the three months ended, June 30, 2016.

BPM Practices in a Japanese Company: A Case Study of Canon Co. Ltd.

Yoko Asakura

Associate Professor, School of International Professional Development,
College of International Professional Development,
Kansai Gaidai University

1. Introduction

The corporate environment has greatly changed over the years. Corporations must rapidly grasp changes in their environment and in their customers' needs and respond to them effectively. Furthermore, corporations need to create customers' needs as well as respond to them in order to gain and maintain competitive advantage. Aligning activities from research and development with the provision of products or services beyond the framework of each organizational unit is important; so is performing activities within the hierarchical structure of an organization to achieve the stated end.

Also, enterprises develop the business globally. They establish and hold the necessary organizational units at appropriate places in the global perspective to accomplish the goal of the whole enterprise. Moreover, they further attempt to develop their businesses by cooperating with entities within their group as well as with other enterprises and utilizing limited management resources more efficiently.

Corporations need to control internal and external activities and even activities beyond national boundaries in order to totally optimize them and achieve effective operations, shorter work hours, and reduce costs. In order to do so, corporations must manage activities on the basis of not only organizations and countries but also each flow of activities. Business processes must be in place to perform the above management.

The term *business process* has been variously defined. According to Hammer & Champy (1993), "the process simply means series of activities that eventually create value for the customer and are needed by each other" (Hammer & Champy, 1993; Nonaka, 1993). And Monden & Lee (2005) state that "the process is composed of dependent multiple-activity groups and explicitly differentiates input from output".

Managing business processes is thought to enable cost reduction resulting from activities that create value, generate more profit, and maximize customers' value. This process management is divided into process management across functions and departments within the enterprise (narrowly defined process management) and process strategies across enterprises and borders (broadly defined process management) (Monden & Lee, 2005, p. 19).

The importance of this process management is explained in Lee (2010). In light of this, in this paper, we will consider how enterprises really execute process management and introduce Canon Inc. ("Canon") as our case study. As is well known, Canon started in the business of developing, manufacturing, and selling cameras and has since expanded its scope of businesses to the fields of office equipment and industrial equipment among others. However, it was not always smooth sailing for the company. Since Mr. Fujio Mitarai became president, however, it has conducted various reforms, made profits, and generated cash flow. It would therefore be meaningful to consider how the company has restructured and managed its processes. Thus, in the sections that follow, we will examine Canon's business development from the perspective of process management.

2. Overview of Canon

Canon was established in 1933 as Precision Optical Research Institute to research an expensive type of small camera and subsequently started business as Precision Optical Industrial Inc. in 1937. In 1955, Canon established a branch office in New York and started to develop business overseas, officially entering the office equipment business. In 1969, it changed its company name to Canon Inc., under which it continues to operate today. Reviewed below is the overall picture of Canon, which is now known as one of the greatest precision equipment makers in the world.

2.1. *Financial performance of Canon from 2011 to 2015*

As of December 31, 2015, Canon's capital stock was 174,762 million yen, and its overall number of employees was around 26,360. Net sales were 2,091,139 million yen for Canon alone and 3,800,271 million yen for the Canon group of companies in the year ended December 31, 2015. Canon had 317 consolidated subsidiary companies and five affiliated companies as of that date. The company's performance in the past 5 years is shown in Fig. 1.

In 2007, having aimed at net sales of 5,000,000 million yen, Canon achieved net sales of 4,481,346 million yen. But Canon's net sales fell considerably to 3,209,201 million yen in fiscal 2009 consequent to the failure of Lehman Brothers in 2008. However, its sales gradually recovered, as Fig. 1 shows. Therefore, Canon has again set this as its target: "it will acquire net sales of 5,000,000 million yen, an operating profit ratio of 15%

	2011	2012	2013	2014	2015
Net sales (millions of yen)	3,557,433	3,479,788	3,731,380	3,727,252	3,800,271
Net income attributable to Canon Inc. (millions of yen)	248,630	224,564	230,483	254,797	220,209
Cash and cash equivalents (millions of yen)	773,227	666,678	788,909	844,580	633,613
Return on Canon Inc. shareholders' equity (%)	9.6	8.7	8.4	8.7	7.4
Number of employees at end of year	198,307	196,968	194,151	191,889	189,571

Fig. 1.   Financial performance over the past 5 years

Source: Canon Inc. (July 31, 2016). Historical Data.

or more, a net income ratio of 10% or more, and a shareholders' equity ratio of 70% or more in 2020" (*Annual Security Report, 2009*, p. 18). Furthermore, Canon has three main business segments: the office business unit, including printers and office multi-function devices; the imaging system business unit, including digital cameras; and the industry and others business unit, including semiconductor lithography and medical equipment. Canon has developed, produced, and sold products in these three business units and has provided service to each set of customers. The production and sales performance of each segment over the 5 fiscal years ending December 31, 2015, is shown in Fig. 2 and Fig. 3.

The following figures show that the office business unit, including printers, has increased production and sales slightly, while the imaging system business unit, including digital cameras, has tended to decrease

Millions of Yen

	2011	2012	2013	2014	2015
Office	1,498,566	1,300,358	1,504,145	1,481,540	1,651,681
Imaging System	1,588,719	1,674,871	1,588,683	1,420,595	1,237,746
Industry and Others	205,288	189,245	159,131	186,080	212,272
Total	3,292,573	3,164,474	3,251,959	3,088,215	3,101,699

Fig. 2.   Production by segment

Source: Canon Inc. (2012), *Annual Security Report 2011*, p. 15. Canon Inc. (2013), *Annual Security Report 2012*, p. 16. Canon Inc. (2014), *Annual Security Report 2013*, p. 16. Canon Inc. (2015), *Annual Security Report 2014*, p. 17.

Millions of Yen

	2011	2012	2013	2014	2015
Office	1,917,943	1,757,575	2,000,073	2,078,732	2,110,816
Imaging System	1,312,044	1,405,971	1,448,938	1,343,194	1,263,835
Industry and Others	420,863	407,840	374,870	398,765	524,651
Eliminations	Δ 93,417	Δ 91,598	Δ 92,501	Δ 93,439	Δ 99,031
Total	3,557,433	3,479,788	3,731,380	3,727,252	3,800,271

Fig. 3.   Sales by segment

Source: Canon Inc. (2012), *Annual Security Report 2011*, p. 15. Canon Inc. (2013), *Annual Security Report 2012*, p. 16. Canon Inc. (2014), *Annual Security Report 2013*, p. 16. Canon Inc. (2015), *Annual Security Report 2014*, p. 17.

Millions of Yen

	2011	2012	2013	2014	2015
Japan	694,450	720,286	715,863	724,317	714,280
Americas	961,955	939,873	1,059,501	1,036,500	1,144,422
Europe	1,113,065	1,014,038	1,124,929	1,090,484	1,074,366
Asia and Oceania	787,963	805,591	831,087	875,951	867,203
Total	3,557,433	3,479,788	3,731,380	3,727,252	3,800,271

Fig. 4. Sales by region
Source: Canon Inc. (July 31, 2016). Historical Data.

production and sales volumes. Digital compact cameras have been on a declining trend in recent years because of the popularization of smartphones with camera functions, resulting in the said decline in production and sales in this business unit. In the industry and other business units, production and sales slightly declined in fiscal 2013 and 2014 but increased in 2015.

Regionally, as shown in Fig. 4, sales in the Americas, Europe, and Asia and Oceania constitute 80% of Canon's sales. In 2015, Canon acquired about 19–30% of the total net sales in each area of Japan, Americas, Europe, and Asia and Oceania. This indicates that Canon has developed its businesses globally.

2.2. Management reforms

Canon conducted various reforms after Mr. Fujio Mitarai became the representative director chairman in 1995. The company began its "Excellent Global Corporation Plan" as a middle- and long-term management plan in 1996. This plan is aimed at making Canon Inc. "really global excellent corporation familiar to and respected by everyone in the world" (Canon Inc. "Middle-Term and Long-Term Management Plan, Excellent Global Corporation Plan").

In the past, Canon had given product development and investment decisions priority over sales. However, since phase I of the plan (1996–2000), the company has begun to manage its own best interests. The company also enhanced its businesses by delisting and merging subsidiaries as well as by selecting and concentrating its businesses. Furthermore, "Canon has carried out thorough management of cash flow by investing only within the range of cash inflow" (Mitarai, 2006, p. 40) to improve its financial standing. Moreover, Canon established management reform committees across divisions, implemented production and development reforms, and so on.

In phase II (2001–2005), Canon worked on "furthering operational reforms in various departments, including development, production, and headquarters management, the enhancement of productivity, and the elimination of waste" (*Annual Security Report, 2001*, p. 17) toward securing "the number-one position worldwide in all of its core business areas". First, Canon stepped up research and development to launch competitive, high-value-added products ahead of their competitors by using unique technology. Canon further reduced costs by targeting the automation of assembly in its production processes. Moreover, Canon enhanced its distribution channels, rationalized its sales organizations, and made a strong effort to diversify businesses in its sales processes.

In phase III (2006–2010), Canon strove to build competitive advantage in its core business areas, launched new businesses, and developed new, farsighted businesses. Further, the company established a new production system for the growth of productivity and built an IT system that summarized diverse information from its whole supply chain for a globally optimized production system. In addition, the company continued to struggle to build its "Three Regional Headquarters" management system for Japan, the Americas, and Europe, which the company had been aiming to do for many years.

Phase IV, which began in 2011, culminated in 2015. This phase focused on the next six strategies of the plan (Canon Inc., *Annual Report 2010*, p. 5):

① Achieving the overwhelming No. 1 position in all core businesses and expanding related and peripheral businesses
② Developing new business through globalized diversification and establishing the Three Regional Headquarters management system
③ Establishing a world-leading, globally optimized production system
④ Comprehensively reinforcing global sales capabilities
⑤ Building the foundations of an environmentally advanced corporation
⑥ Imparting a corporate culture and cultivating human resources befitting a truly excellent global company

In phase IV, Canon aimed at expanding the businesses to related and peripheral businesses by improving and innovating conventional products. The company reinforced the medical imaging, industrial equipment, and network camera sectors as new business domains. Furthermore, the company set out to establish the Three Regional Headquarters management system with the Americas and Europe on the basis of the existing research and development system in Japan. Besides, the company pushed forward with a globally optimized production system to "seek to deploy bases and allocate the amount of production to minimize cost and risk from a comprehensive view, including currency exchange, the tax system, working power, procurement, distribution, and so on" (*Annual Security Report, 2011*, p. 16). The company tried to organize sales methods and systems for both emerging and developed countries.

As mentioned above, Canon has launched numerous management reforms. These include improving and restructuring its production and distribution processes. In the following sections, we will consider process management in the context of Canon's production and distribution.

3. Production Reforms at Canon: Process Management

3.1. *Cell production system*

Domestic and international manufacturing companies organized in headquarter and each business have produced products in Canon. Since 1998, Canon has switched from a production system using conveyor-belt machinery to a cell production system ("cell production"), which is "a production system in which relatively skilled assembly workers are grouped by one or several workers, and the groups assemble mass-produced parts into finished products customized and accommodated to demand trends in the market" (Tanzawa, 2001, p. 82).

This cell production started in Nagahama Canon Inc. ("Nagahama Canon"), a subsidiary of Canon's. Nagahama Canon, producing laser printers, toner cartridges, and so on, launched the production reform at the end of 1997 and started cell production in 1998. This reform was very successful, significantly reducing cost and subsequently spreading to each division at Canon. Canon finished the shift toward cell production in

October 1999 and pulled out conveyor-belt machinery from all its factories around the world in 2002.

Canon managed to considerably reduce costs and increase production efficiency using cell production. First, Canon did not need to make significant initial capital investment; it merely emptied the space occupied by the conveyor-belt machinery. Hence, the company was able to utilize the empty area effectively for other purposes. Furthermore, each team member not only worked in his or her own designated capacity but was also able to support preceding or following processes because the company switched to cell production by each team. This further resulted in each cell increasing its productivity (Editorial Department of President Inc., 2004, p. 103).

Canon was able to flexibly respond to various changes in demand because all processes were conducted by individuals or small groups in cell production. Moreover, the company transferred members who excelled in cell production to other departments, including the development departments. In addition, the company tried to streamline processes beyond the framework of departments by incorporating the production department's opinion into the design processes.

Now, Canon has taken cell production to a new phase — the "man–machine cell" production system. Oita Canon Inc. ("Oita Canon") has been using this system since 2005. Oita Canon manufactures interchangeable-lens digital cameras, digital camcorders, and suchlike. This system has evolved from cell production. "The company placed automated equipment and measuring instruments between work teams in cell production and achieved more productivity than existing cell production" (*Earnings Briefing 2010*, 2011, p. 7).

Oita Canon tripled its productivity of 10 years ago through the introduction of this production system. Alternatively, "Oita Canon could have reduced the number of workers in the production line of the cameras' main bodies. Therefore, Oita Canon has more self-manufactured parts than ever before and transferred the workers to other departments, including manufacturing technology departments" (*Weekly Toyo Keizai*, 2014, p. 92). Canon continues its efforts to mechanize the production system toward more efficiency.

Canon has brought a new dimension to cell production. The system has also had a ripple effect on operations other than production.

Mr. Hisashi Sakai, president of Canon Electronics Inc., stated, "Converting to the cell production system has changed the method of development and sales and the system of stocks. Canon got great effectiveness because of this synergy" (*Nikkei Monozukuri*, 2007, p. 97).

Cost reduction through improvement of the production process is limited. Therefore, Canon improved and changed various processes throughout the whole value chain within the enterprise, including distribution, as described below, in order to utilize the transition to cell production. In concrete terms, it may be said that Canon got the following result from the transition to cell production: "Canon had introduced supply chain management and shortened the work-in-process inventory turnover period from 24–25 days to 4–5 days. Again, the company had shortened its parts inventory turnover period from 3–4 days to 6 hours because of the introduction of a just-in-time system" (Mitarai, 2006, p. 41).

3.2. Total optimization in Canon's factories: Nagahama Canon Inc.

As already stated, Canon sought to make production processes more efficient through accomplishing breakthrough production reform of cell production. Canon tried to optimize the whole plant from the perspective of distribution to make the production reform more effective. In other words, Canon tried to optimize the process of accepting parts, manufacturing products through various stages, and shipping out finished products beyond the function of production. This optimization was present in Nagahama Canon, which started cell production.[1]

First, Nagahama Canon started the project of distribution reform in 1995. Because of this project, "Nagahama Canon had started 'factory banning' to deliver products from factories directly to customers without going through the distribution center. Factory banning means directly delivering products from the factory for the company" (*LOGI-BIZ*, 2003, p. 42). This enabled Nagahama Canon to streamline the process from factories to customers.

---

[1] 3.2 is compiled on the basis of the following article. *LOGI-BIZ* (2003).

In addition, Nagahama Canon was able to review the flow of goods in the production process by introducing cell production, so it was receiving parts and shipping products that the company started to review first. In other words, "receiving parts is the process of providing parts to the cells for assembly. On the other hand, shipping products is the process of loading up delivery tracks with finished products" (*LOGI-BIZ*, 2003, p. 43). It is supposed that the company launched the streamlining of operations other than the assembly operation because it tried to make the assembly operations more efficient by utilizing cell production.

Nagahama Canon made the flow of operations rectilinear and simple and also streamlined the production process because its existing production used conveyor-belt machinery. However, the flow of production became complex because by introducing cell production, the company assembled parts in smaller groups. Therefore, the company first decided to change the layout of the factory. In fact, Nagahama Canon made the transition to a layout in which they could effectively receive parts and ship products in line with the cell production system.

Moreover, Nagahama Canon decided to think about the effectiveness of not only receiving parts and shipping products but also the flow of workers and goods in cell production to optimize all operations in the factory. The company came to use the following approach in this effectiveness: "Nagahama Canon makes distribution more of a priority than production. The approach is to review the production method itself to realize a smooth distribution" (*LOGI-BIZ*, 2003, p. 44).

In fact, Nagahama Canon decided to "improve the movement of assembly operation in cells along the macro flow" (*LOGI-BIZ*, 2003, p. 44) in the layout of the factory, which they had changed earlier. The production departments had suitably resisted this method because this change presupposed major alterations on the production departments.

However, Nagahama Canon prepared the structure for it to be capable of performing in 2002 and formed the project team. The company changed the structure of the cell and finished changing the factory layout within 6 months after the company started the team. This project was promoted through six stages (*LOGI-BIZ*, 2003, pp. 45–46):

① Raising awareness
② Organizing the workplace

③ Consolidating inventory
④ Rectifying the flow of workers and goods
⑤ Cycling the operation
⑥ Developing tools to eliminate waste of operations

First, Nagahama Canon created an environment in which things of little use would not be put in the workplace and requirements would be used quickly. Using this method, the production operation proceeds effectively. Moreover, the company decided to consolidate inventory into two places, not to disperse it. This improvement facilitates the acquisition of knowledge of the volume of inventories by members of cells at all times, effectively making them refrain from increasing wasteful inventory.

In addition, Nagahama Canon reviewed the layout of the cells, identified the causes of action running counter to the macro-flow, and "shifted the layout of cells to the form of 'I' to keep the workers' action constant" (*LOGI-BIZ*, 2003, p. 46). Next, the company created a system in which as few workers as possible would manufacture products. In other words, the company created a system that repeats part of the operation at a constant pace so that workers could perform the operation in time according to the speed of production without wasting motion. Finally, the company developed the tools necessary to conduct the production process effectively and eliminate waste.

"Nagahama Canon succeeded in reducing 30% of the number of delivering workers in the factory and 18% of the parts inventory by the improvement of distribution" (*LOGI-BIZ*, 2003, p. 46), which is in line with the above discussion. It is conventionally important for mainly production departments to reform a production process. However, when the company reviewed the movement of workers and goods within the production process, it realized that these actions were wasteful. Therefore, the company focused on how to eliminate wastage in the flow of workers and goods while maintaining the effectiveness of production. This system enabled them to cut the distance and time involved in moving workers and goods and to reduce inventory.

"Canon reduced costs totaling 311 billion yen (including the effect of development and procurement reforms in fiscal 2004) for 7 years from fiscal 1998 to fiscal 2004 and became the representative excellent earnings enterprise of Japan through these production reforms" (*Nikkei Information*

Strategy, 2005, p. 54), including the abovementioned restructuring of business process, which translates to cell production.

Cell production, the shift toward the man–machine cell production system, and the associated effectiveness of production processes represent process management within the company beyond the functions from purchasing to sales distribution. Such management allowed Canon to optimize the processes of not only the main operations, including production and sales distribution, but also the support operations. This is in keeping with the narrowly defined management of processes in the very definition of process management. The company has tried to optimize processes across functions and departments within the company.

4. Globally Optimized Production System and Cooperation with Other Enterprises: Process Strategy

4.1. *Process management beyond national boundaries*[2]

As already stated, 80% of Canon's sales have been from overseas pursuant to the development of its globally optimized production system. The company had to install production bases in optimal areas, looking beyond borders, to realize this globally optimized production system. Each base had to be deployed with the streamlined processes of the whole company, from research and design to logistics — the overall value chain in the company. Canon had to deploy each base and allocate production to it to minimize cost and risk. For example, the company needed to create a system in which research and development departments developed products that matched the needs of customers, manufacturing departments performed in response to demand, and sales departments delivered products to customers in a timely manner when they required them. This enabled the company to maximize value for customers.

Canon has mainly developed and designed products in Japan. Thus, the company planned to increase production bases in Japan near the development and design bases to optimize the processes of the whole enterprise across borders. This made communication between development and

---

[2]4.1 is compiled based on the following article: Fukumori (2013).

production bases easy. Moreover, development and design bases could perform production-process-conscious activities, and production bases could produce products considering the development and design base's intention. This would enable Canon to create a synergy effect.

Furthermore, when Canon reviewed the value chain in the whole company with a global perspective, they determined that it was important to not only streamline development and production processes but also cut the lead time of distribution to the customer in the whole business process and to reduce costs. "Canon has not had distribution subsidiaries, has set up the integrated logistics center (the 'integrated center') as a department under the president, and has implemented all operations at headquarters. The integrated center has operated and managed logistics across all businesses at Canon and pursued the most appropriate logistics in the whole company" (Fukumori, 2013, p. 3). In other words, the integrated center at the headquarters aims at optimizing distribution in the overall company along with designing logistics appropriate to each business at Canon.

In terms of conducting all operations associated with logistics on its own, Mr. Fukumori, chief of the integrated logistics department, stated, "The purpose of performing the logistics operations on their own is to communicate with each business smoothly, perform the operations quickly, and launch an independent attack to improve business processes and heighten productivity of operations" (Fukumori, 2013, p. 3). As Canon reviews the logistics of the whole company, it must globally pursue the optimization of the value chain in each business as well as the overall company. In particular, the company organizes the system to easily communicate and is likely to get local information by sending the integrated center's personnel to domestic and overseas sales companies and production bases. Moreover, in the event of problems, Canon can respond quickly because the company manages all logistics operations within the enterprise.

As Canon reviews its distribution process now, it needs to consider not only reduction of costs but also environmental problems. Thus, the company must spread the word that optimization at Canon can reduce carbon dioxide in the overall logistics process while also cutting costs.

When Canon examines the establishment of a new production base to achieve this goal, the integrated center comes into play in the initial stages. Canon decides where to establish a new base upon considering the accomplishment of a globally optimized production system with regard to logistics.

Canon deploys the development, manufacturing, and sales bases keeping its sights trained on the world as a whole and coordinates the activities of each base so that it can play its role. The company builds up the system to ensure the accomplishment of total optimization by managing the logistics process within the company across the world. It is thought that the company consistently considers restructuring its global business process from the viewpoint of total optimization, which leads to the effectiveness of the whole enterprise.

4.2. *Process management beyond enterprises: Collaboration between companies*

Canon has restructured its business processes beyond the enterprise framework as well as within the enterprise. In concrete terms, the company has both outsourced domestic distribution and realized the collaboration of the function by cooperating with other corporations.[3] This collaboration started as a project between Canon Marketing Japan Inc. ("Canon MJ"[4]), a subsidiary of Canon, and Epson Sales Japan Corp. ("Epson Sales"), a sales subsidiary of Seiko Epson Corp. ("Epson"). Further, Nippon Express, Inc. ("Nittsu"), responsible for distribution, has joined this project, and Nittsu Research Institute and Consulting, Inc. ("Nittsu-Soken") was involved in the project as a coordinator. In addition, Konica Minolta Business Solutions Japan Co., Ltd. (currently Konica Minolta Japan, Inc.), ("Konica Minolta") has participated in the project since 2012.

Canon and Epson have held much the same market share and had similar distribution problems. Moreover, Nittsu had mainly performed distribution for these two companies. Both companies could organize a

---

[3]4.2 is compiled on the basis of the following articles. Ishinabe, K. (2011), *LOGI-BIZ*. (2014), Inoue, H. (2014), Katayama, N. (2014).

[4]Canon MJ holds Canon Business Support Inc. (Canon BS) which sets up a shared service business as subsidiaries. Canon BS actually plans and performs domestic distribution operations (Ishinabe, 2011, p. 28).

cooperative system of distribution led by Nittsu because Nittsu was familiar with both operations of distribution.

They set the following three goals for this project (*LOGI-BIZ*, 2014, p. 20): "① delivery of products to electronics retail stores", "② collaborative delivery to client companies in each area", meaning products can be brought in and tooled up on the ordinary delivery route for small- and middle-delivery destinations, including offices, and "③recovery of used toner cartridges".

Both companies have delivered products to much the same electronics retail stores and by the charter services based on the retail stores' terms of delivery. However, the shipping weight of the charter services was not enough, and both companies experienced wastage. Therefore, they achieved great effectiveness by jointly delivering products. The project now encompasses Japan as a whole for the areas in which collaboration is deemed effective.

Next, they extended the range, mainly in big cities, for collaborative delivery to each area. In this delivery service, they collectively delivered products to customers in certain areas. "Owners of products can have the advantage of better delivery services as well as the effectiveness of cost reduction by utilizing the existing distribution infrastructures and manpower in the distribution service provider that actually collects and delivers the products" (Katayama, 2014, p. 26) because of this service. In other words, Canon not only outsourced distribution operations to Nittsu but also enjoyed the services jointly with other companies. By employing this method, Canon utilized the management resources of Nittsu and Epson and reduced its costs. Additionally, Canon made the operations more efficient.

Moreover, this collaboration enables them to recover used toner cartridges when delivering products. In a normal delivery system, they could never have recovered used toner cartridges. They can reduce operations by this delivery system.

With this project, they proceeded with sharing warehouses used to deliver products. This shared use of warehouses has run along smoothly because their warehouses are in proximity to each other or they use the same warehouses. They have improved their effectiveness because this shared use of warehouses enables them to share storage areas and perform delivery operations in parallel.

Various considerations are necessary, however, because this collaboration requires cooperation with other competitor companies. They need to objectively coordinate the project in view of the rationality of the overall project because difficulties in collaboration are created when each company defends its own perspective. Nittsu-Soken plays a role to coordinate the project. It can perform optimal operations as a whole because Nittsu-Soken adjusts its opinions.

As shown above, Canon could accomplish cost reductions in delivery operations as well as effectiveness of operations by linking delivery operations that it performs on its own to other companies' operations. In addition, the company can reduce the number of deliveries as a whole because of the collaborative delivery arrangement. Thus, the company could achieve reductions in carbon dioxide emissions, thereby fulfilling corporate social responsibility in terms of reducing the effects of its actions on the environment.

5. Conclusion

In this paper, we considered production and distribution reforms on the basis of the processes that are currently employed in Canon.

First, Canon utilized a production system with conveyor-belt machinery but then switched to cell production, which allows the company to respond to customers' needs quickly and make operations more efficient. Moreover, with the introduction of cell production, the company streamlined production processes internally from the perspective of distribution. The company restructured a production process in the manufacturing industry. This restructuring was performed on the basis of a flow of workers and goods rather than on that of an operation in production. This restructuring enabled the company to reduce workers and inventory. The company could use limited management resources effectively by transferring workers to other departments. This restructuring allowed the company to reduce unnecessary inventory than before and costs as well. The company maximized customer value and cost reduction by optimizing its business processes beyond internal functions and departments.

In addition, Canon developed cell production — the man–machine cell production system, in which part of the production operations in a cell is automated to enhance effectiveness. The company can reduce time and cost and promote correctness when the operation is mechanized.

Furthermore, the company aims to optimize activities in the whole company globally. Logistics on the global perspective plays a considerable role in optimizing activities. The company seeks the optimal logistics strategy in consideration of the overall value chain because the integrated center manages the logistics of all businesses. The optimal logistics contains the assignment of each base to the optimal area. The center offers an advantage because it is within the company and moves closely together with each production base and sales company. Through this cooperation, Canon reduces its logistics costs in the whole company and pursues total optimization of logistics that delivers products when they are required.

Finally, Canon outsourced distribution operations in the past as well but has now done so in collaboration with other corporations to obtain a big benefit or outsources parts of the processes that are beyond the framework of its enterprises. In addition, the company has been in cooperation with other companies that perform similar operations to make the operations more efficient. This enables the company to aim at streamlining operations and reducing costs. Moreover, the company can reduce carbon dioxide emissions in the fulfillment of its corporate social responsibility.

As observed above, Canon manages processes over functions and departments within the company and optimizes processes within the company (even beyond borders). In addition, the company performs the selection and concentration of processes and cooperates with other enterprises beyond the framework of the company. It is thought that Canon has tried to review and streamline business processes from various views, even external to the company and its departments. The company will need to review the optimization of the overall supply chain from various perspectives regardless of the size of the processes and make an effort to create maximum value at minimum cost.

References

Asakura, Y. & Kimura, A. (2010). BPM Practices in a Japanese Company: A Case Study of Canon Co. Ltd., *Business Process Management of Japanese and*

Korean Companies, Singapore: Lee, G., Kosuga, M., Nagasaka, Y. & Sohn, B. (eds.), Chapter 6. World Scientific Publishing Co. Pte. Ltd.

Asakura, Y., Sakate, K., Nagasaka, Y. & Kimura, A. (2007). Field-site Transmitting BPM: A Case Study of Canon, *Sanken-Ronsyu* (Kwansei Gakuin University), Vol. 34, pp. 11–20 (in Japanese).

Canon Inc. (2002). *Annual Security Report 2001* (in Japanese).

Canon Inc. (2003). *Annual Security Report 2002* (in Japanese).

Canon Inc. (2004). *Annual Security Report 2003* (in Japanese).

Canon Inc. (2005). *Annual Security Report 2004* (in Japanese).

Canon Inc. (2006). *Annual Security Report 2005* (in Japanese).

Canon Inc. (2007). *Annual Security Report 2006* (in Japanese).

Canon Inc. (2008). *Annual Security Report 2007* (in Japanese).

Canon Inc. (2009). *Annual Security Report 2008* (in Japanese).

Canon Inc. (2010). *Annual Security Report 2009* (in Japanese).

Canon Inc. (2011). *Annual Report 2010*.

Canon Inc. (2011). *Annual Security Report 2010* (in Japanese).

Canon Inc. (2011). *Earnings Briefing 2010* (in Japanese).

Canon Inc. (2012). *Annual Security Report 2011* (in Japanese).

Canon Inc. (2013). *Annual Security Report 2012* (in Japanese).

Canon Inc. (2014). *Annual Security Report 2013* (in Japanese).

Canon Inc. (2015). *Annual Security Report 2014* (in Japanese).

Canon Inc. (2016). *Annual Report 2015*.

Canon Inc. (2016). *Annual Security Report 2015* (in Japanese).

Canon Inc. (July 31, 2016). Historical Data. http://www.canon.co.jp/ir/historical/index.html. *The Information for Investors in Canon* (in Japanese).

Canon Inc. (July 31, 2016). Middle-Term and Long-Term Management Plan "Excellent Global Corporation Plan", http://www.canon.co.jp/ir/strategies/concept.html. *The Information for Investors in Canon* (in Japanese).

Canon Inc. (March 14, 2016). The History in Canon. http://web.canon.jp/corporate/history/. *The Company Information in Canon* (in Japanese).

Fukumori, K. (2013). The Literature: The Efforts of Global Logistics in the Canon, *LOGISTICS SYSTEMS*, Vol. 22, pp. 2–5 (in Japanese).

Hammer, M. and Champy, J. (1993). *Reengineering the Corporation: A Manifesto for Business Revolution*, New York: HarperBusiness.

Inoue, H. (2014). Learn from the attack of Canon and Epson: Part II — Why Can They Continue the Project? *LOGI-BIZ*, Vol. 14. No. 3, pp. 22–25 (in Japanese).

Ishinabe, K. (2011). The Challenge of Canon and Epson, *LOGI-BIZ*, Vol. 10, No. 12, pp. 28–31 (in Japanese).

Iwamuro, H. (2002). *The Cell Production System*, Nikkan Kogyo Shimbun, Ltd. (in Japanese).

Kajiwara, Y. (2009). The Successful Methods of Cooperative Delivery between Same Industry—Toyobo Co., Ltd. & Teijin Fiber Ltd., Seiko Epson Corp. & Canon Inc. & Nippon Express, Inc., and Food Service Industry & Minaminihon Total Logistic Service, *LOGI-BIZ*, Vol. 9. No. 7, pp. 28–31 (in Japanese).

Katayama, N. (2014). Learn from the attack of Canon and Epson: Part III — The Mechanism That the Companies Develop the Attack, *LOGI-BIZ*, Vol. 14, No. 3, pp. 25–29 (in Japanese).

Lee, G. (2010). The Conceptual Framework of Business Process Management, *Business Process Management of Japanese and Korean Companies*, Singapore: Lee, G., Kosuga, M., Nagasaka, Y. & Sohn, B. (eds.), World Scientific Publishing Co. Pte. Ltd.

LOGI-BIZ. (2003), Case Study: Nagahama Canon: The Improvement of the Point of Production, Vol. 3, No. 6, pp. 42–46 (in Japanese).

LOGI-BIZ. (2014), Learn from the attack of Canon and Epson: Part I — Partnership with Competitors, Vol. 14, No. 3, pp. 20–21 (in Japanese).

Mitarai, F. (2006). The Interview with Mr. Fujio Mitarai: The President of Canon says, The Groundwork up to 2010 to Make Canon Last for 100 years to 200 years", *Nikkei Information Strategy*, Vol. 14, No. 12, pp. 38–42 (in Japanese).

Mitarai, F. (2014). The Command to return the production to Japan to 50% of Domestic Production Ratio, *Weekly Toyo Keizai*, 6516, p. 93 (in Japanese).

Monden, Y. & Lee, G. (2005), Conceptual Framework and Management Accounting of Process Management, *Accounting*. Vol. 58, No. 5, pp. 18–32 (in Japanese).

Nagahama Canon Inc. (July 31, 2016). Outline and Corporate History. http://www.canon-nagahama.co.jp/company/index.html. *Company Information* (in Japanese).

NATURE INTERFACE (2003). The Front Line of Environmental Business: Forward the Compatibility between Management and Environment in Canon (First Part), Vol. 14, pp. 80–82 (in Japanese).

Nikkei Information Strategy. (2005). The First Condition to Become Real-World Learders: The Strength to Reveal Subordinate Capabilities, Vol. 14, No. 11, pp. 54–56 (in Japanese).

Nikkei Monozukuri (2007). The President of Canon Electronics Inc., Mr. Hisashi Sakamaki "The Role of Frontline Workers and Responsibilities of Top Management" pp. 96–97 (in Japanese).

Nonaka, I. (1993). *Reengineering Revolution: Operating Innovation that Radically Change Enterprises*, Nikkei Inc. (in Japanese).

President Inc., Editorial Department (2004). *The Rule of Canon: The Working Method of Salaried Employees to Earn Much Money*, President Inc. (in Japanese).

Tanzawa, Y. (2001). "The Cell Production System" in Canon Office Equipment Inc. *The Monthly Bulletin of Social Science*, Vol. 457 and 458, pp. 82–84 (in Japanese).

Weekly Toyo Keizai (2014). The Production Method to Combine "Hand Working" and "Automation": "Man–Machine–Cell Production System" that Canon tests, 6516, p. 92 (In Japanese).

BPM Practices in a Korean IT Service Company

Kyounghwan Cha
Managing Consultant, IT Service Co. Ltd.

Seungchan Lee
Managing Consultant, IT Service Co. Ltd.

Suyong Kim
Senior Consultant, IT Service Co. Ltd.

Hyunjong Yoo
Assistant Consultant, IT Service Co. Ltd.

1. Introduction

A Korean Information Technology Service company (Company A) was established in 1989, and it currently ranks top class in its domestic industry. The company operates from consulting to system integration, system maintenance, IT outsourcing, as well as various Information and Communications Technologies (ICT)-based convergence business and related services. Recently, the company expanded their business globally, which takes around 20% from the shares of the company's total revenue. Company A mainly focuses on business-to-business (B2B) and has been running by a standardized manual. In other words, they seize business opportunities that can be developed as future solutions. Although most companies already possess their own standardized working processes, the majority of businesses are formalized. Although there are numerous cases that cannot adopt a standardized process set because of recent changes in business circumstances, most cases are being performed with somewhat standardized process sets. More than 10,000 contracts are being received annually throughout small to big businesses. Company A, one of the leading companies in the domestic IT industry, has already been proceeding with business standards establishment and establishing the business process management (BPM) structure for a decade.

In the following, we introduce the background of this study, the approach measure of BPM, BPM project procedures detail, and achievement of BPM adaption through company A's project.

2. Background and Approach

The company started paying attention to the BPM structure due to the rapid growth of awareness regarding the importance of "operational efficiency". In the past, company A had no standardized working processes and connectivity among sales, service delivery, and support division because there were no such support systems such as Business Process Management System (BPMS). At the same time, just as in other countries, Korean business industries were highly interested in advanced enterprise portals (EP), workflow, and BPM. Following these trends, company A also decided to take a huge step in innovating the entire operating system. In order to do so, they proceeded with the following approach methods, along with overall consulting tasks. Regarding the situation of company A, they had tried to perform process innovation (PI) for optimizing the overall business operation. To do so, they had approached the following BPM method with internal overall consulting processes.

2.1. *Definition of BPM in company A*

Company A defines BPM referring to automation, integration, optimization between inner- and outer-business processes, so as to make (1) business process efficient and (2) a continuous activity of enhancing enterprise value.

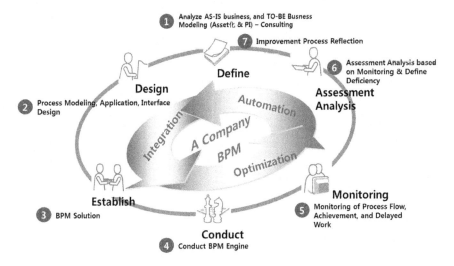

Fig. 1.   A company PI cycle based on BPM

Note: "The enterprise BPM Flow" refers to BPL Planning Consulting Task of Korean Home Appliances 2006.

To innovate the business process, company A (1) defined the entire business process and the existing unit of tasks as unit of processes, (2) extracted end-to-end (E2E) processes connected to the core processes of the company, and, finally, (3) determined priorities among the processes for managing them thorough BPM in a smooth process flow.

Additionally, they had approached with an aspect of an automation by a system.

3. Performance Stage Details

3.1. *Enterprise process set establishment*

The first stage in establishing enterprise process efficiency based upon BPM is to define what tasks exist in a company and what processes are following these tasks; this activity is called "define the enterprise process set". To establish the structure of enterprise process efficiency, the first step is identifying the enterprise process set. The basis of improving the activity is in the visualization of the entire task process and subsequently applying concrete improvement measures and the BPM structure.

Fig. 2.   Process set management structure based on BPM

Source: Company A's BPM task result report 2010.

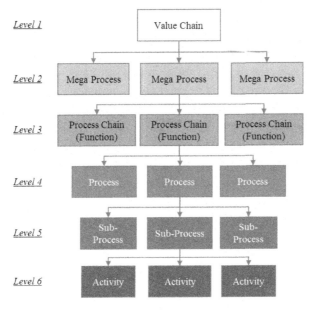

Fig. 3.   Process set structure

Table 1.   The initial process set status in company A

Classification	Process group	Process	Sub-process
Business plan	15	57	200
Business perform	20	73	259
Business support	35	233	1,012
Total	70	363	1,471

Company A, in the first stage, mainly focused on clarifying the overall structure of the business system. It categorized its business processes into six levels. The components of level 6, activities (tasks), were extracted by drawing the "process map" in the "process innovation" stage (see Fig. 3).

For BPM automation processes based upon workflow, all tasks, including activity levels and the business system, needed to be structuralized and visualized. As such, company A, in the early stage, defined enterprise process sets as 3 mega processes, 70 process chains (Process Group), 363 processes, and 1,471 sub-processes, along with the structure in Table 1. Additionally, sub-processes comprised of activities.

After structuralizing the entire process set, they proceeded to extract E2E processes through workshops with work-site operators for realizing the workflow-based BPM system in the future. The BPM-applied E2E process was selected by the criteria on daily process, process that should done within a short period, process that has numerous labors, and process be that is needed for automation. Therefore, if they scored higher on a certain process, they required more labor for setting priorities (five-point rating scale and five evaluation criteria: occurrence cycle, processing time, frequency of process, number of labor, and need for automation). As a result, 13 E2E processes pertaining to the entire business were chosen and the priorities of applying BPM into certain processes, along with the above evaluation, were set. Consequently, the company established a standardized sequence of process flow from discovering business opportunities to the completion of a project after procuring B2B business contracts, which is considered the core of company A.

3.2. *Core business PI*

An overall innovative project takes around 5 months, including structuralizing the entire process set selection of the E2E process (to apply BPM). The consultants established the appropriate path to support the PI process, while the operators on the work-site took the lead, because they needed to work with every department, such as finance, accounting, judicial affairs, procurement, business planning, IT. The PI method, led by the consultants, was to visualize the chosen E2E process. In other words, the process map which covers up to activity level (level 6) was preferentially drawn and finalized the altered "to-be process map" and "process dictionary", together with work-site operators and consultants. Fig. 4. shows the logic flowchart of the tasks in the PI process "process map". The guideline of this process map was prepared by the consultant and performed by work-site operators.

Additionally, the following logic flow diagrams and the points of analyzing the process were provided to a user performing a PI process, and it helped progress it with the consultant (see Fig. 6).

The PI process does not only improve the process but also realigns the necessary asset tasks. This was a work of specification for the future system, which contains the BPMS. Specifically, because BPMS runs by an

After defining the Process Set, Find an Opportunity for improvement Process with a various analyses

Process Set Define

- Define Mega Process/ Analysis of other process' effects (Scope, Terminology, Index etc.)
- Define Process Owner
- Process Dictionary and Standardization

Process Analysis

- Analysis of Each Process
- Analyze effect of other Process
- Input/output Analysis
- Process Map should be done parallelly

Process Improvement Process Set Reflection

- Improvement Define
- Best Practice Adoption
- Establish To-Be Model
- Process Reflection

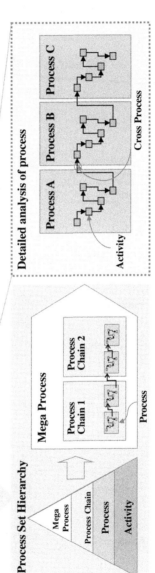

Process Set Hierarchy

Mega Process
Process Chain
Process
Activity

Mega Process

Process Chain 1
Process Chain 2

Process

Detailed analysis of process

Process A
Process B
Process C

Activity

Cross Process

Fig. 4.   Process analysis

Cross-Process Analysis for inter-Process connectivity analysis with Process composition analysis(Activity), Input/Output Analysis

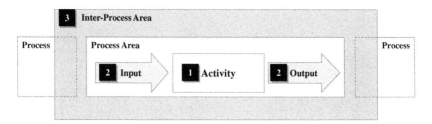

1	Activity	2	Input/Output	3	Inter-Process
① Eliminate the Redundant, unnecessary Activity/ Divide, Integrate Activity ② Activity Conduct Analysis ③ Decision Logic Analysis		④	Input/Output Analysis	⑤	Cross-Process Analysis

Fig. 5.   Cross-process analysis

Source: Company A's BPM task result report 2010.

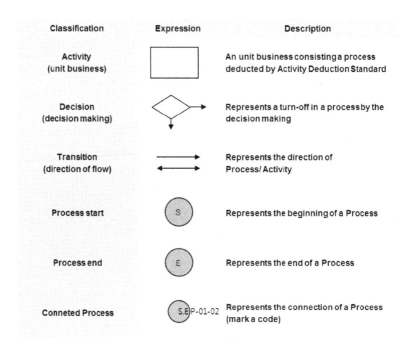

Fig. 6.   The components of logic-flow for PI

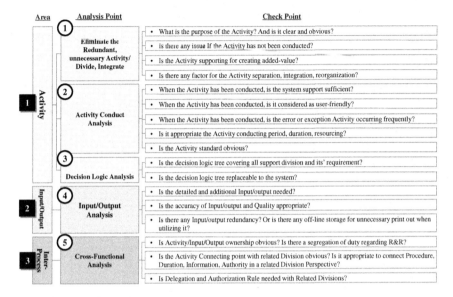

Area		Analysis Point	Check Point
1 Activity	①	Eliminate the Redundant, unnecessary Activity/ Divide, Integrate	• What is the purpose of the Activity? And is it clear and obvious?
			• Is there any issue If the Activity has not been conducted?
			• Is the Activity supporting for creating added-value?
			• Is there any factor for the Activity separation, integration, reorganization?
	②	Activity Conduct Analysis	• When the Activity has been conducted, is the system support sufficient?
			• When the Activity has been conducted, is it considered as user-friendly?
			• When the Activity has been conducted, is the error or exception Activity occurring frequently?
			• Is it appropriate the Activity conducting period, duration, resourcing?
			• Is the Activity standard obvious?
	③	Decision Logic Analysis	• Is the decision logic tree covering all support division and its' requirement?
			• Is the decision logic tree replaceable to the system?
2 Input/Output	④	Input/Output Analysis	• Is the detailed and additional Input/output needed?
			• Is the accuracy of Input/output and Quality appropriate?
			• Is there any Input/output redundancy? Or is there any off-line storage for unnecessary print out when utilizing it?
3 Inter-Process	⑤	Cross-Functional Analysis	• Is Activity/Input/Output ownership obvious? Is there a segregation of duty regarding R&R?
			• Is the Activity Connecting point with related Division obvious? Is it appropriate to connect Procedure, Duration, Information, Authority in a related Division Perspective?
			• Is Delegation and Authorization Rule needed with Related Divisions?

Fig. 7.   The checkpoint for process analysis

automatized system that designs and takes actions, rules and policies should be precise and clear. Figures. 8 and 9 represent the PI to-be image and process dictionary written during the PI process.

3.3. Realization of PI via BPMS

Practically, performable BPM processes were realized through improved processes in the PI project, and the smooth flow between each process was considered as well. To perform BPM process, it had to be defined first: the standards of performing tasks, roles and responsibilities (R&R) of users who performed the task, and communication, etc. Therefore, they carried forward the adaption of the BPMS system based upon workflow to make the process flows and results visible.

Process Criteria for BPMS

— The Process, which should be done within a certain time frame;
— The Approval Process, which was already defined by delegation and
     approval authorization;
— The Process, which should be monitored by workflow status.

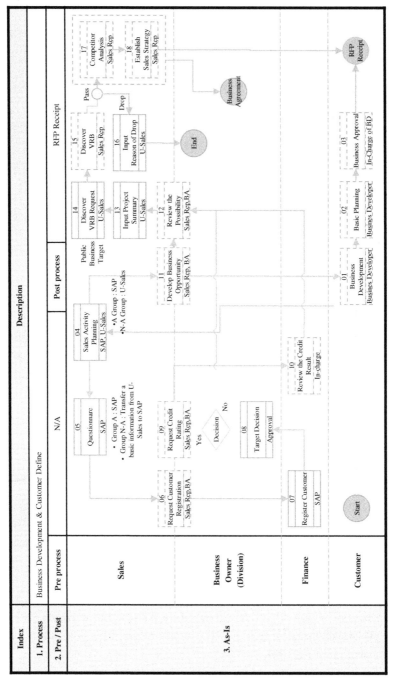

Fig. 8.　Process map (sample)

1. Basic Information	Process Structure	Project Op. & Mgmt + Account Op. Mgmt. + Biz Development & Client Relationship Mgmt. > Business Development > Agreement						
	Process Code	OOO-01-01	Name of Process	Sales Agreement			Version	1.0
	Division	PI TFT	In-Charge	OOO	Date	OOOO.OO.OO	Reviewer	UUU
	Process Owner	Business Sales Team		IT				
2. Process Definition	Description	Verify the Project Code after reviewing and signing the final agreement, which was written during the negotiation.						
	Owner	Business Sales Div, Business Development Div		Supporting Div	Fianace, Business Planning, Legal Supporting Div			
	Pre- Process	Prepare the agreement and insurance		Post Process	Billing, Project Kick-Off			
	System	Sales, SAP, Accounting, Contract		Task Manual				
	Cycle	Frequently		Frequency	Around 330 time / Month			
	Duration	Contract Period		Execution	Frequently			
	Input	Agreement Template, Negotiation of Condition		Output	Final Agreement, CP, Project Code, Win- Loss Analysis			
	Remarks	New Report						
3. Process KPI	Index	Metric	Result	Goal	Description (Formula)			
	Review the contract	Time			The Time from the request of Legal Support team to reply			
	Contract confirmation by SAP	Time			After entering the agreement, duration between inputting the order to Sap and confirming the contract.			

Fig. 9.   Process dictionary (sample)

Select the process by the criteria priority above and apply it to the BPM process.

The process, which was selected based on the above criteria, was applied to BPM with a definition of the business flowchart based on the workflow.

3.4. BPMS-Application

In the PI stage, it is necessary to realign the process-flow based on the workflow, which performs a system-driven task, to apply BPMS purposing the practical automation of processes and adopt generally improved processes into the present system. In other words, the concept of workflow needs to be defined precisely. It is a nominal approach by which system developers and consultants draw the workflow together. Fig. 11 shows how to design the process using the workflow tool. It may look simple, but the activities are performed through ERP or relative business systems. As an activity proceeds, it will be shown to the next operator through a "to-do list" or "approval" via EP, since each activity is automatically linked to appropriate main operators, according to PI results.

As such, the process automation-based BPM system is established after processes visualization through PI, which was designed by

BPM Selection Process

> Assessment Criteria

1	Frequency	Daily ...
2	Processing Time (Time/Metric)	Short Period..
3	Amount of Transaction	A bunch of Transaction..
4	Participants (per transaction)	With many ....
5	Automation Needed	Puch Function, Reduction of Manual working,,,

> BPM Priority for Process Adoption

No	Process	Frequency	Process Time	Transaction	Participants	Automation	Final Assessment
1	Outsourcing	4.20	4.20	4.20	3.00	3.80	3.88
2	Purchasing	4.82	4.18	3.36	2.36	3.64	3.57
3	SM Service	4.14	4.29	3.79	2.64	2.86	3.54
4	Post SI Project	3.73	2.82	3.36	3.00	3.91	3.36
5	Sales Contract	4.31	3.13	3.38	2.38	2.63	3.16
6	Asset Mgt	3.23	3.92	3.15	2.38	2.92	3.12
7	SI Porject	4.52	3.90	3.00	2.43	1.71	3.11
8	Retirement	3.50	4.50	3.50	1.50	1.00	3.00
9	Recruit	3.15	3.73	3.12	2.19	2.04	2.85
10	Finance & Closing	3.00	3.55	1.55	1.36	4.00	2.69
11	Company Strategy	1.65	1.90	1.20	3.75	2.10	2.12
12	Business Strategy	2.37	2.00	1.68	2.95	1.53	2.11
13	Marketing	1.81	1.75	1.25	2.50	1.00	1.66

Fig. 10.   BPM selection process

Source: Company A's BPM task result report 2010.

workflow, BPMS engine embedment, and connection of systems. Regarding users, they progressed in an inefficient manner, for instance, pre-operators transfer a completed task to post-operators via e-mail, phone call, or messenger before applying the BPM system. Subsequently, the post-operators went through cumbersome processes to conduct business by implementing independent ERP systems or relative task systems. However, ongoing tasks are automatically assigned to appropriate main operators via EP in the new BPM system.

Fig. 12 shows all employees conduct business using EP, such as sending e-mails, approving requests, and utilizing Knowledge or Collaboration. Specifically, a list of tasks assigned to an appropriate operator would be shown via the "To-Do" tab and could be performed one by one by clicking task lists in the system. Under the standardized processing system, a user is able to check the status of tasks via "Process Flow", noting the result of a processed task, such as where a bottleneck occurs and how fast a task is ongoing. Moreover, employees who are not familiar with their task can utilize task assets, such as relevant task manuals, templates, and documents by clicking a corresponding activity. Through the business system improvement, company A could have a better business environment, which makes performing numerous tasks rapid and precise.

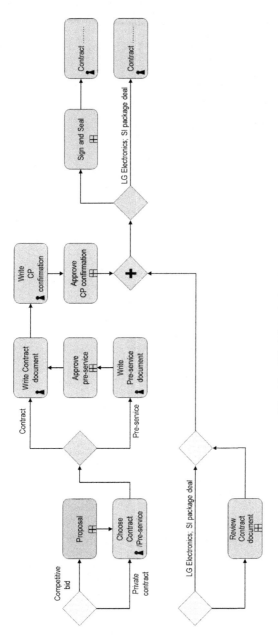

Fig. 11. Workflow design (sample)

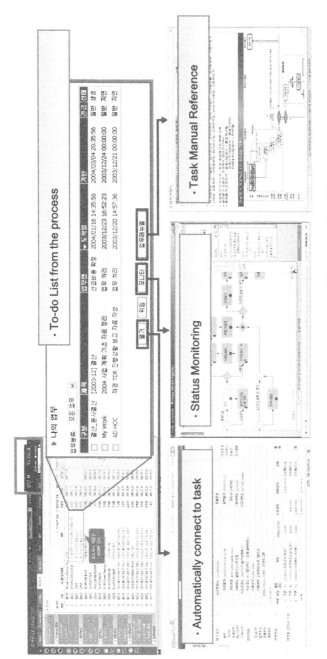

Fig. 12.   Work processing via EP under BPM system (sample)

Improve internal Customer Satisfaction	Reduce the Transaction time and effort by system support and improvement of Process Efficiency
Improve Organization Capability and Quality	Improve the Organization Capability and Quality by establishing Rule base System and Process
Enhance external Customer Satisfaction	Response to customer's requirement quickly by enhancing the internal process. It can provide a high quality result to external Customer
Improve Co-working Process with Partners	Improve Co-working Process with Partners by strengthening communication process and channel
Compliance with Business Ethics	Compliance with a legal and business ethic rule by Process monitoring

Fig. 13.   Expectation effect

Source: Company A's BPM task result report 2010.

4. Company A's Adoption of PI and BPMS

A company could improve its organization capability and work quality by adopting PI and BPMS and enhance the satisfaction of internal/external customers and partners. Additionally, company A could prepare a basic guideline of compliance processes for business ethics.

5. Conclusion

Although company A had an advantage in standardization due to the nature of its business, the company implemented a basic approach of the BPM system in a timely manner, which led to successful adoption of the BPM system without any trial and error. Specifically, a powerful commitment from board of directors in leading the change was the key success factor in this case.

This case has been considered as a success story of implementing the BPM system. Especially, the fact that work efficiency was maximized by connecting to the EP is a good example. For a company considering a successful BPM implementation, the methods and approach used in company A would be an adequate reference. This does not consider the simple systematic approach; a company should set the goal of process automation from the perspective of business and process optimization. Additionally, it is also important to have the technical maturity to work with systems such as ERP. In the case of company A, except for the approaches listed above, related working systems were modified significantly. The entire process had taken slightly over a year although disruptions were not considerable.

PART III

Action Research of BPM in Japanese Small and Medium-Sized Enterprises

Methodology of Business Process Management for SMEs

Gunyung Lee

Professor, Niigata University, Japan

1. Introduction

The IT era has changed competitiveness in today's business world; competition no longer exists between large and small companies, but rather, between those that are either prompt or tardy. The company that shares information is more successful in this changed world than the company that manages information. Process management, which strengthens cooperation between a thing (material, goods in process, or product, among others) and information flow across an organization, is necessary to survive and succeed in such a changing business environment. Many studies have recently been conducted on this subject; simultaneously, constant developments and innovations occur in the Business Process Management (BPM) software field. However, due to the many specifications that companies and developers attempt to incorporate into a single software program, the IT tools available today have become increasingly complicated and unwieldy. As a result, IT tools, which should ideally assist corporate management, have essentially become black boxes that cannot be easily referenced. The execution of these IT tools is even more difficult for Small and Medium-sized Enterprises (SMEs), as insufficient management knowledge exists of business flow, funds for process construction, and human resources for management.

Therefore, this paper will study the BPM model, which unites management and BPM's construction methodologies, as appropriate for SMEs. This paper will first discuss the BPM's conceptual framework for SMEs, followed by a gradual process construction and process management theory.

2. Event-Driven Business Process Management (ED-BPM) and Business Model

A company typically employs multiple, varied techniques to resolve its issues. However, these techniques often cannot achieve desired outcomes despite expending considerable time and resources on developing them, and they are not used again. Therefore, many techniques are not in use due to the inefficiency of the techniques themselves, as opposed to their not having adapted to a changing environment. A company's original business model must adapt to changes in the business environment to survive among today's high competition. It is necessary, in other words, for a company's business framework, which uses its internal and external management resources efficiently, to be built and executed based on the market's expectations and demands that accompany environmental change.

Dowdle *et al.* (2003) suggests that a technique's success depends on how the technique is introduced, how it connects to the organization's philosophy, and how it supports the current strategy. They insist that a business model must clearly define its connection to *philosophy*, *methodology*, and *tool*, according to organizational hierarchy. Thus, a specific business model's success in an SME context must clearly define the market's expectations; harmonize business operations and market demand; and provide organizational philosophy, management methodology, and management tools, which are components of the business model that should be managed.

This study aims to arrive at a business model that evaluates the organization by adapting the *performance management of horizontal organizations* as philosophy, the *Event-Driven BPM (ED-BPM) model* as methodology, and *SCRUM*[1] as an IT tool, and by providing solutions

---

[1] SCRUM is introduced by Matsumoto (2017) of this volume.

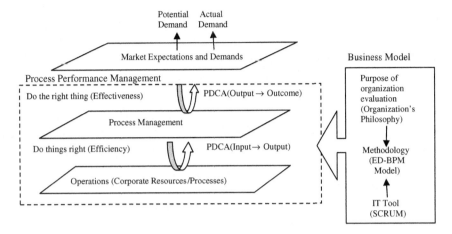

Fig.1.   Components of a business model

(Fig. 1). Additionally, the company must customize its process management system to have streamlined operations that respond effectively to
the market's expectations or demands. This customization will require
incorporating management indicators in the business model to the competitive environment. On the other hand, it is imperative that process
management incorporates twin principles: *do the right thing* (or the
macro-management of the relationship between output and outcome)
and *do things right* (or the micro-management of the relationship
between input and output).

3. Construction and Management of the Process, based on ED-BPM

The concept of BPM refers to "the control and management of transactions between organizations both within and outside corporations by
viewing the transaction flows as processes, which is enabled by breaking up the traditional walls between organizations, sharing information
and resources among them, and combining and connecting their
transactions" (Lee *et al.*, 2009). Ease of process construction and the
simplicity of process management are dual requirements of a BPM in
the SME context. This study proposes a BPM model, called ED-BPM,

to build a BPM model that fulfills such conditions and is relevant for SMEs.

3.1. *Process construction and deployment through event*

The first step when building a process involves clarifying a process entrance and exit points, and expressing and building a process as a chain of simple tasks or activities. It is important that this be conducted in advance; once a process has been built, considerable effort is required to modify it at a later stage. Additionally, the resources, time, and effort required to modify a process could be two or three times more than those taken to build it. A key concept to consider at this stage involves an *event*, or is the cause, driver, or trigger to form and execute a process. This process execution is initiated by the start of an order, which embodies an event, and a process is ultimately formed by this event, as aforementioned. If mountain climbing is considered as an example, trailheads would correspond to events, and the individual and group mountain-climbing visitors, according to each trailhead, would correspond to an order.

When building a process, it is also important to clearly define beforehand the relationship between these three factors: the *event, process*, and *task*. A *process* is a frame that represents a series of workflows and is built from a chain of two or more work units (tasks). Although a process is a unit of grouped tasks, this does not require any action through work instructions. A *task* refers to the minimum unit of work that must be handled. A workflow can be represented by tasks, and a *start* and *end* are identified for each task. Simultaneously, one task can be redefined as a sub-process by further decomposition. One sub-process in such a case can consist of a chain of two or more tasks. In other words, when one task or minimum unit is further decomposed into multiple tasks, this is known as a sub-process or a chain of two or more tasks. Fig. 2 illustrates that Task 1 in a parent process starts with an event. After the operating activity directed by Task 1 is completed, the work moves to Task 2. If a manager wishes to manage the detailed operating activity in Task 1, the parent process task can be further decomposed, and a child process will be built and executed. Namely, Tasks 1–1 and 1–2 are executed instead of Task 1, and the work then moves to Task 2.

Parent Process

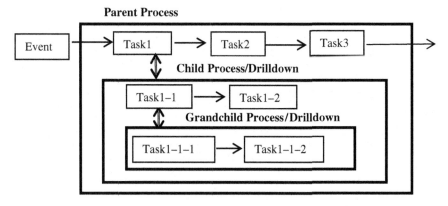

Fig. 2. Process drilldown

3.2. *Matryoshka doll model*

An analogy can be drawn between the process construction under the ED-BPM, suitable for SMEs, and a Matryoshka doll, Fig. 3 demonstrates that only one simple doll (parent process), such as the Russian doll, is initially built; the parent process completes Level 1 of process management. If a manager wishes to manage the contents of the doll (or the process) in detail, a drilldown approach can consecutively build inner dolls (child and grandchild processes) and improve management accuracy. This is represented in Fig. 4.

3.3. *Process management based on ED-BPM*

The ED-BPM methodology manages and improves processes using relevant data acquired from SCRUM, an IT solution (Fig. 5). The ED-BPM uses not only a staged process construction methodology through the drilldown approach detailed in Section 3.2, but also a staged process management methodology, considered as an appropriate process management technique for SMEs.

This study considers three kinds of process losses, which must be appropriately managed by ED-BPM and eliminated:

Waiting loss: this refers to the loss occurring due to a delay in the flow of information between demand and production, and between usage and procurement.

Fig. 3.   Parent process

Fig. 4.   Drilldown of process

Efficiency loss: this refers to the loss that occurs due to a lack of management within an operation, or between multiple operations.

Organization loss: this occurs due to structural impediments faced within an organization. Typically, this leads to complicated decision making, which hampers the ease of operations within the organization.

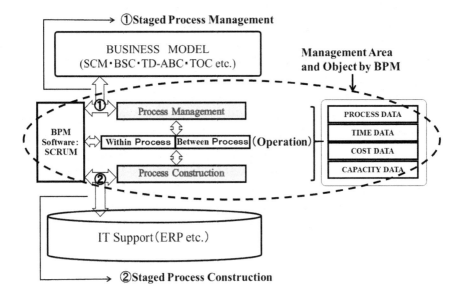

Fig. 5. Staged process construction and management

The ED-BPM methodology is built according to the *unit process* principle, which is capable of decomposing the complete operational flow of a horizontal organization. This is a simple and an effective methodology that manages a process outcome from the perspectives of time, cost, and process inventory. Some of its salient features are as follows:

(1) Understand the operating process in a horizontal organization as an *activity chain due to an event.*
(2) *Visualize* an operating process with IT support.
(3) Understand and evaluate the target for process management as a *process loss.*
(4) Promote *performance improvement* using information on an operating process' *time, cost, capacity, and process inventory.*

4. Staged Process Construction and Management for SMEs

The staged application of process management is desirable in SMEs due to restrictions in funds and/or human resources. An organization decides on an introductory level of process construction and management methodology according to its internal process management conditions. Once it has verified the methodology's outcome, the methodology must advance to the next level. If this study's methodology is applied, and if an attempt is made to visualize process losses using information on time, cost, capacity, and process inventory, then process losses will be eliminated and corporate performance will improve. This study considers that it is more effective to build a process by stages for process management in an SME context. The *parent process* (first layer process) is built in the first stage, and the parent process' losses are actualized by *visualizing* the process. Bottleneck tasks, yielded by the parent process' losses, are decomposed and the sub-processes, or the *child process* layers (second layer processes) are built. Processes are thus simultaneously improved and refined; if necessary, a process can be further decomposed to a *grandchild process* layer (third layer processes), and activities are conducted to eliminate the process loss.

4.1. *Staged process management and elimination activities of the process loss by process drilldown*

A clear distinction must be made between the elimination activities of the process loss by process drilldown, and multi-staged process construction and management. An organization cannot first build the process at a company level and then subsequently manage the process. It is imperative to create a balance between process constructions that spans multiple departments in a horizontal organization, and includes the drilldown of bottlenecks in each process, which may directionally differ. This study takes an original approach, in which a process is built and managed in stages, as per the company's internal requirements (Fig. 6). Such an approach greatly differs from the currently available IT solutions. An approach commences in ED-BPM to minimize process losses, in which a clear demarcation is made between: (1) the direction that aims at process systematization, and (2) the direction that aims to increase efficiency by the process drilldown. Once this demarcation is complete, a management measure is established against each of these two components, which subsequently advance in stages.

Process Systematizing Level

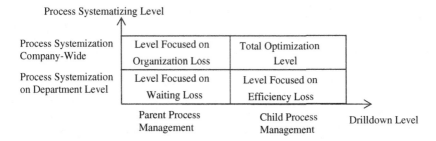

Fig. 6.   Staged process management in SMEs

An initial step performed at the ED-BPM introduction stage involves minimizing the impact of waiting losses during process construction and management. As detailed earlier in the study, a waiting loss occurs when a time lag occurs in the flow of information within a department or process, or between the company and the market. Therefore, process time is measured and holding time is minimized to understand, analyze, and eliminate waiting loss. Once waiting loss has been eliminated, it is necessary to decide a further direction: whether a process is now considered as systematized, or whether it must be further decomposed. If efficiency loss has been given priority over waiting loss, then the bottleneck in the built process is further decomposed in an attempt to increase the process' efficiency. An efficiency loss occurs when inefficient factors exist within a process and the difference of the capacity between processes. Therefore, both process time and process cost must be measured to understand, analyze, and eliminate efficiency loss, and to conduct cost improvements. A company prioritizes the minimization or elimination of organizational loss, as this is necessary to extend process construction at a company level, and to conduct company-wide management changes. An organizational loss occurs when an absence or insufficient cooperation occurs between a company's primary and support departments. Therefore, process time and inventory must be improved to understand, analyze, and eliminate organizational loss. Irrespective of the priority and direction selected by an organization, process management that strives for total optimization will eventually eliminate the three process losses and is considered important.

4.2. *Staged performance management based on ED-BPM*

This study addresses management through the methodology of multi-staged systematization and process drilldown. The approach *visualizes* the current condition of the process and eliminates *process loss*. This approach, in other words, improves corporate performance by eliminating waiting, efficiency, and organizational losses.

The method of eliminating process loss in stages is also desirable, as SMEs have limitations in funds and/or human resources. The methodology, if necessary, advances to the next stage only after we construct and manage a simple process (parent process), and its outcome is confirmed.

This study will discuss the method of building and managing a process in the following sub-sections by: (1) the elimination of waiting loss by simple process construction; (2) the elimination of efficiency loss; (3) the elimination of organizational loss; and (4) total optimization.

4.2.1. *Elimination of waiting loss*

In the first step of a process construction and management, one single process is structured at a departmental or functional level. The *parent process* construction in a horizontal organization can help the company map the complete value chain by using the scale of *time*. For example, in a call center's troubleshooting process, the activity time is measured for each task in the process. The value-added activity time and waiting time for tasks can then be analyzed (Moinuddin *et al.*, 2007).

4.2.2. *Elimination of efficiency loss*

The second step of a process construction and management involves analyzing the bottlenecks in the parent process built in Step 1; we deploy a child process through a detailed drilldown. As only by drilling down a parent process to a child process, the respective activity times of the parent and child processes can be compared and a detailed waiting time can be measured. This drilling-down process also enables the calculation of costs for each task activity. Time-Driven Activity-Based Costing (TD-ABC) is also considered as an effective cost-calculating method, in addition to traditional cost accounting methods. Moreover, methods known as management techniques by cost per time, such as Throughput Accounting (TA) and Time-Based Accounting (TBA), are considered appropriate for this model. The calculation and management of appropriate costs is achieved in these methods by efficiently applying each method's feature, as the task's activity time is used as a driver that distributes cost. The purpose and the cost accounting calculation under each method are summarized as follows:

(1) TD-ABC

Kaplan & Anderson (2004) proposed TD-ABC to solve the issues associated with conventional ABC, using performing-a-task time as a driver, instead of transaction drivers, such as issue purchase order or customer request, of conventional ABC. The TD-ABC approach connects department costs to an object in cost accounting through an activity chain process. A process cost is calculated by multiplying the process fulfillment time by the time unit cost of the department cost. This is a simple model, which can calculate the cost of an object in cost accounting by providing an intrinsic process cost against an order or a customer. Although the process time is measured by the observation of activity, or through an interview in TD-ABC, further discussion is necessary regarding how to measure process time, including the method used by this study (Lee & Nagasaka, 2011). Although this study does not apply an equation that the TD-ABC uses, the basic concept is similar.

(2) TA

TA is based on the Theory of Constraints (TOC), a system of management thinking (Golddratt, 1990). The TOC is a system-improvement methodology that identifies a system's constraints that obstruct goal achievement and discovers ways to overcome them. A process in the TOC is improved by focusing on the bottleneck or the constraint (limited resources). Although *throughput = sales − material costs* is the basis of TA, the product mix is decided under production capacity limitations using the throughput concept. An organization faced with production capacity limitations should handle the usage time of its bottlenecked limited resource as a cost driver. The organization should calculate and compare the time costs by product and maximize its throughput. The measurement of time in TA is relatively simple, as it focuses on the time used by both a limited resource and a product.

(3) TBA

The TBA methodology uses a product's manufacturing lead time as a basis for distributing manufacturing overhead (Hutchinson, 2007). Each product's average lead time is measured under TBA, and the total lead time calculated by multiplying it with a budget volume of production. The total manufacturing overhead is divided by the total lead time, the allocation cost per lead time is established, and the manufacturing overhead is accordingly allocated to its products. The lead time is the time used from the start of the manufacturing process to its completion, including the time utilized to correct any mistakes (Takahashi, 2001). The manager under TBA continuously focuses on decreasing the lead time and reducing costs. The shortening of lead time immediately improves customer response time, resulting in increased opportunities for profitability improvement (Takahashi, 2001). Although the measurement of lead-time in TBA is relatively simple, an analysis may be required of the process used to shorten it. Fig. 7 summarizes the utilization of time as a cost driver for each of the aforementioned methods.

This study first applies TA, but no bottleneck resources are applied in this accounting method. Manufacturing costs, excluding material costs,

	TD-ABC	TA	TBA
Cost Element for Decision	Full cost	Materials cost	Full cost
Cost Driver	Activity time	Usage time of limited resource	Lead time
Method of Cost Accounting	Activity time × (departmental cost/total activity time)	(sales–materials cost) /working time of limited resource	Direct cost + (manufacturing overhead/lead time)

Fig. 7.   Features of the cost accounting and management of time-based techniques

are treated as an operating cost. Note that the operating cost is divided by the capacity time of a fixed period. Therefore, this study will adopt a method that uses operating cost per time for both cost accounting and cost control.

4.2.3. *Elimination of organization loss*

From a value chain perspective, the existing process between main departments can manage both time and costs. However, to harmoniously manage the complete value chain process, the support department processes must also be adjusted and controlled. Congruence, in other words, must exist in the processes of both the support and main departments, and as a result, the bottleneck in a management chain, Plan–Do–Check–Action (PDCA) becomes clearly visible. Such a bottleneck can be eliminated by improvements in the decision-making process. At this time, the process inventory data becomes important for further improvements.

A process is divided into main and support processes. The main process refers to that which changes the worth of the product or service that has been built for the external customer through transformation and multiplication. The support process, as the term suggests, is any process that supports the main process. Support processes also include various operations that manage activities that may not directly contribute to satisfying the external customer's demand (IMA, 2000).

An organizational loss occurs when the main and support processes intricately connect the structure. Therefore, a process for inventory control is necessary after establishing a process management unit to enable the management chain's function, to incorporate inventory within and between processes as well as eliminate process inventory.

4.2.4. *Process management for total optimization*

Finally, a drilldown of the bottleneck in each process is also performed while building company-wide processes. If company-wide process management is successful, the company can obtain a wealth of information regarding various processes, which enables it to further improve each of them.

5. Process Management Model by Time Information in ED-BPM

This study aims to build a practical ED-BPM model that reflects the results obtained from the action research performed on two Japanese companies to solve process management problems. Therefore, this proves the model's availability and practicability, although a need exists for further modification. Specifically, this model centers on time information about the process and on management using time as a driver. This model's structure is suitable for SMEs, as the time and process information measured with the SCRUM IT tool can be analyzed in Microsoft Excel. The following three points are applicable in this model's time information aspect:

(1) Time
     Process management is performed by measuring and applying time within a process and between processes, such as lead time and working hours. For example, this enables delivery time management by order, the improvement of process working hours, and inventory control, among others.

(2) Timing
     The estimated time and profitability information are used in real time. For example, this enables delivery time management as well as estimated cost accounting using an expected time.

(3) Speed
     The volume of production and the cost based on time-by-product is managed using the process outcomes between and within a process as well as the outcome per time. Although existing techniques were introduced that involve cost accounting or cost control using time information, such as TD-ABC, TOC, and TBA, this study uses the analysis frame as detailed in Section 5.1 and applies it in Microsoft Excel.

5.1. *Assumptions for applying ED-BPM*

First, Table 1 illustrates that the purchase orders are A1 and A2, and it is assumed that A1 had a purchase order of 250 and A2 received a purchase

Table 1. Profitability management by order in ED-BPM

Order Lead time (hours)

Order No.	Number of orders	Process 1	Process 2	Waiting time	Total time	Quantity per time	Sale price	Production amounts	Direct material costs	Throughput amounts
A1	250	30.5	48.8	10.2	90	2.8	400	100,000	30,000	70,000
A2	200	32.4	40.0	13.6	86	2.3	450	90,000	27,000	63,000
Total		62.9	88.8	23.8	176			190,000	57,000	133,000

Allocated Operating Costs

Throughput per time	Process time costs	Waiting time costs	Total costs	Estimated gross profit	Gross profit per unit	Profit speed	Unused capacity rate	Unused capacity costs	Gross profit-unused capacity costs
782	24,781	3,188	27,969	42,031	168	470			
733	22,625	4,250	26,875	36,125	181	420			
758	47,406	7,438	54,844	78,156			45.16%	45,156	33,000

order of 200. Second, it is assumed that the total manufacturing lead times for each order are 90 and 86 hours, respectively. As the waiting time between tasks can be measured in this model, each waiting time, or 10.2 hours for A1 and 13.6 hours for A2, becomes the target for process improvement as waiting loss.

5.2. Product information per time and process analysis by throughput

If it is assumed that the sale price of A1 is $400 and the sale price of A2 is $450, then the total value of production will be $100,000 ($400*250) and $90,000 ($450*200), respectively. Alternatively, if the direct material costs of A1 and A2 are assumed to be $120/product unit and $135/product unit, respectively, the throughput amounts deducted as direct material costs from the total production amounts change to $70,000 ($100,000–$120*250) and $63,000 ($90,000–$135*200), respectively. Under the TOC, after calculating throughput amounts per time of limited resources, the manufacturing of products will be prioritized by the throughput amount per time. However, as no precondition of constraints exists in this study, only the throughput amount per time of manufacturing lead time is calculated. The calculations indicate that the throughput amount per time of A1 is the largest. If the throughput per time were the only measure of profitability, A1 would be considered more profitable for the company than A2, as the former has the largest throughput per time. Further, the production volume of the product per time of A1 and A2 is measured as 2.8 and 2.3 products, respectively. Thus, the production volume and throughput amount per time of each product indicates that A1 is superior to A2.

5.3. Elimination of process loss by cost information per time

The operating cost per time is calculated by dividing the manufacturing overhead (as used in TBA) or the operating cost (as used in TOC) by lead time under the following assumptions; the allocated amount of the operating cost by order is also calculated.

Assumptions:

* Total available labor-time for 1 month
= 2 workers × 8 hours a day × 20 days per month
= 2 × 8 × 20 = 320 hours

* The total operating costs for 1 month
= $100,000

Therefore, the operating cost will be $312.50 (100,000/320) per time. If the total working hours by order are applied, the operating cost allocated by order will be calculated. Thus, the operating cost of A1 will be $27,969 and the operating cost of A2 will be $26,875. The operating costs deducted from throughput amounts by order gives us $42,031 as the profit of A1, and $36,125 as the profit of A2. Moreover, if the profit per time unit is calculated by dividing profits by lead time, the profit per time for A1 would be $470 and that for A2 would be $420. Thus, the superiority of gross profit on sales per product unit by order over gross profit on sales per time by order is reversed. This is because A2 has greater productive time, although its profit margin is greater than that of A1. Thus, we can posit that if no limited resources exist, such as in this case, the profit per product unit becomes the criterion by which we judge profitability. However, if resources are limited, the profit per time of the limited resource becomes a criterion by which we judge profitability. Process improvements would need to be conducted considering the relationship between such time and cost information.

Alternatively, if the unused capacity applied in TD-ABC and its cost are calculated, we find that the total unused capacity is 45.16%, and the cost is $45,156. In other words, 54.84% of the workers' available labor time is used. If this unused labor time is represented as a cost, it comes to $45,156. As this amount is a cost that is not allocated to products, it must be deducted from the company's overall profits. As a result, the real gross profit on sales is $33,000 when we deduct unallocated but incurred costs, or the distribution variance, of $45,156 from the estimated gross profit on sales, $78,156. Thus, we observe that such a calculation framework can provide useful decision-making information to SMEs. Additionally, time information can be used for process improvement as well as to estimate profitability. Note that in this model, all purchase costs, such as material costs, are treated as incurred costs at the time of purchase. Therefore, from a financial perspective, although the amount of material inventory is calculated by the cost percentage method for the current period, the amount of material inventory is placed under the heading of incurred current costs for the purpose of cost management. It is also noteworthy that such a calculation method for the purpose of cost management is similar to the calculation method in *Amoeba Management* (Inamori, 2013) in Kyocera Corporation, or in the TOC.

6. Conclusion

Today's competitive environment is one of turbulence: an age of instability, discontinuity, and uncertainty. A company in such an environment must be prompt in its decision making in cognizance with the changing environment, and it cannot rest on its past successes alone. A company's top management must always monitor the changing environment, devise his strategies accordingly, and accept the consequences of his plans. However, the introduction of a company's vertical strategy, which uses a top-down approach, frequently results in information gaps. These arise between various functions and departments, resulting in insufficient cooperation between them, which affects strategy implementation. Process management in a horizontal organization becomes important to manage such a situation.

Although the model proposed in this paper imagines process construction within a single company, process construction between companies is also possible using the same method, as the model is extendible to a substantial degree. Although process inventory control has not been studied in detail in this paper, the management of process inventory using the lead time, or the product and the cost information per time, is important. The process inventory includes the inventories of a thing (materials, goods in process, the product, etc.) and of information (management inventory of documents, etc.). For example, 7-Eleven convenience stores collectively recognize that management that minimizes missing sales (opportunity loss) and eliminates leftovers from sales (abandonment loss), forms the fountainhead of profits (Takeuchi, 2001).

References

Dowdle, P., Stevens, J., Mccarty, B. & Daly, D. (2003). Process-Based Management: The Road to Excellence, *Cost Management*, pp. 12–19.

Golddratt, E. M. (1990). *Theory of Constraints*, North River Press.

Hutchinson, R. (2007). Linking Manufacturing Strategy to Product Cost: Toward Time-Based Accounting, *Management Accounting Quarterly*, pp. 31–42.

IMA. (2000). *Implementing Process Management for Improving Products and Services, Statements on Management Accounting No.4NN*, Institute of Management Accountants, April, pp. 11–13.

Inamori, K. (2013). *Amoeba Management: The Dynamic Management System for Rapid Market Response*, CRC Press.

Kaplan, R. S. & Anderson, S. R. (2004). Rethinking Activity-Based Costing, *Harvard Business Review*, Vol. 82, pp. 131–138.

Lee, G., Kosuga, M. & Nagasaka, Y. (2009). The Usefulness of Business Process Management in Cost Management, *The Journal of Cost Accounting Research*, Japan Cost Accounting Association, Vol. 33, No. 1, pp. 18–27 (in Japanese).

Lee, G. & Nagasaka, Y. (2011). The Expansion and Simulation of Time-driven Activity-based Costing based on Business Process Management, *Korean Accounting Journal*, Korean Accounting Association, Vol. 20, No. 4, pp. 259–286 (in Korean).

Moinuddin, K., Collins, T. & Bansal, A. (2007). Process Activity Mapping: Activity-based Costing for Semiconductor Enterprises, *Cost Management*, pp. 29–33.

Takahashi, K. (2001). Study on Cost Allocation based on Time, *Yokohama Kokusai-Kagaku-Kenkyu*, Vol. 16, No. 3, pp. 311–321 (in Japanese).

Takeuchi, Y. (2001). A Change and Management Control of Strategic Management, *Kigyo-kaikei*, Vol. 53, No. 5, pp. 27–33 (in Japanese).

Development of Event-Driven Business Process Management (ED-BPM) Tool "SCRUM"

Hiroyuki Matsumoto

Representative Director, 956 Inc.

1. Introduction

For large or small companies and various industry types, a business visualization tool is a killer solution in keeping the business healthy and sustaining growth. For example, an Enterprise Resource Planning (ERP) system is utilized in global companies, and all employees interact with the system. The system stores job information for each employee. Directors may use the system for various business decisions. The ERP system is enormous because all data for various business roles [business logic, footage, human resources (HR) related, etc.] are stored within it.

For Small and Medium-sized Enterprises (SMEs), a business visualization tool is an important solution that helps achieve goals and maintain the business. However, an ERP system is not suitable for most SMEs at a certain point of system scale and cost.

At the beginning stage of business visualization, a paper and pen is utilized to record results of each job. At the end of the day, a line manager collects all results and approves them as the daily report. However, Internet Technology (IT) tools are a better choice in that they alleviate some of the stress for workers and managers caused by manually recording the day's activity. However, there are several problems in using IT tools.

- *Cost (infrastructure development, maintenance staff)*
- *IT literacy of all users*

In this paper, I introduce a business visualization tool for SMEs and give an example of its installation in an actual company.

2. Introduction to SCRUM

SCRUM is a software that originated from a discussion in an "ED-BPM small and medium-sized company" study group. The software has several time measurement features for business workflows. The latest version, SCRUM PRO 4, is used in several industrial companies.

SCRUM provides two types of User Interfaces (UIs): the first is called device view, and the second is called admin view. Device view, for example, may be used by a machine operator, while admin view may be used by a line manager or director.

Using the device view, when an operator chooses an option, SCRUM records details such as the following:

- *Task Name and Type (Production, Break, Maintenance, etc.)*
- *Start and end time, and duration*
- *Person in charge*

A key difference between ERP and SCRUM is that ERP provides a company-wide business logic platform to ensure that whole processes are correctly performed. Any task that is not defined in the system cannot be executed. SCRUM, however, focuses on recording all events that are actually performed, including exceptions and errors. If a critical situation arises in the production area, SCRUM does not provide any information to assist operators for error recovery. The system only records the start time and duration of the situation.

3. Basic Design Concept

SCRUM was developed as a Business Process Management (BPM) tool used for SMEs; however, it is different from typical ERP systems and other process management systems. Following are some key features of SCRUM.

3.1. *Process definition using graph model*

A graph model is a data model used to represent a network topology. This model represents network phenomenon by using two elements: node(s) and edge(s). SCRUM uses a graph model to represent workflow. Here, workflow is a collection of a series of tasks, with a fixed order and execution control for each task (see Fig. 1). Nodes represent a work item, while edges link these work items to each other and provide two types of connection attributes — upstream and downstream — to represent the execution order of the workflow series.

As the workflow must have at least one starting point, the nodes have an attribute that indicates a start point. Additionally, the connection points have connection state attributes such as "branch (downstream)", "fork (downstream)", "aggregation (upstream)", or "queue (upstream)". In the workflow definition of SCRUM, there is no logic like conditional branches, etc. Assessing whether the workflow is suitable for business use is always the decision of the business; there are few regulations required for incorporating specific conditions into the workflow. Through the connection structure of each node, the workflow definition can be sufficiently simplified.

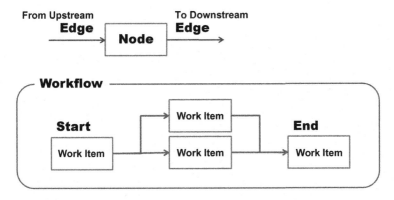

Fig. 1. Graph model and business workflow

Such concise representation may be disadvantageous when expressing a complex workflow (for example, when it is required to concurrently perform different tasks depending on conditional branches). SCRUM suggests the workflow should be extensible and simple rather than all encompassing. For such workflow representation, SCRUM provides two techniques such as event-driven process patterns and drill down structure, both of which will be described later. SCRUM does not prompt the system to build a detailed workflow from the beginning; it proposes defining processes by hierarchy and accumulates small portions of the workflow.

3.2. Event-driven process

Consider the situation of an order received from a customer in which an appropriate workflow is involved. In SCRUM, the workflow execution model involves an occurrence of a "trigger (event)" followed by the related "workflow (process)". As each product has a different manufacturing workflow, it will have an independent manufacturing process definition associated with it that includes work items (tasks) and links unique to a particular product.

If an order for product A is received, the event for product A and associated process is initiated. Here, the event and process are independent, hence, generic workflow operations can be performed. However,

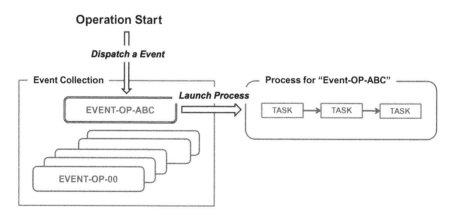

Fig. 2.   Event-driven process

where product A and B have different specifications, yet the same production workflow, a new event is added for product B and associated to the product A process. If some differences exist in the workflow, we define and associate a new event and process for the new product.

Further, for unexpected tasks, such as machine maintenance or breakdown, an operator will interrupt the current working task and switch to the maintenance task immediately. Such a situation may occur over several tasks and add too much complexity to the workflow series. SCRUM provides an internal event mechanism to support such unexpected situations. First, several maintenance events and their associated processes are defined in SCRUM. Then the events (internal events) are associated to the task with the unexpected work situation. If a machine breaks down, the respective internal event will be initiated and associated process will be carried out. Following the completion of the unexpected task process, the machine will return to the normal process.

Sometimes, you can find some commonality when you examine a process. The internal event mechanism provides a method to define an effectively simple solution for such a situation.

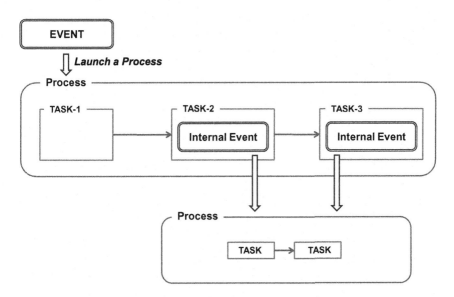

Fig. 3.   Internal event mechanism

3.3. Drill down

We consider the example of a situation where an order is received from a customer. To process the order, a series of tasks need to be performed, such as the following:

- *Tasks in the production control division*
- *Tasks in the manufacturing division*
- *Tasks in the delivery division*

If you consolidate whole tasks in several divisions, the configured workflow becomes enormous, leading to high installation costs. This is one of the disincentives of the ERP system installation. To reduce the installation costs, SCRUM provides a drill down feature. This function enables further disintegration of the original task into sub-processes (child processes).

In the above situation, the process will be created as a departmental level process by simply connecting one to three tasks of each division. The "Top-Level" process form is very simple. The drill down feature provides a method that can be extended when you need to see a detailed workflow at any time.

There is no limit to the number of drill down levels. In other words, a process to which the drill down function has already been applied may be further broken down to more levels. This approach is particularly useful in the following cases:

- *Businesses can deploy this process vertically to define workflow for each granular level of the organization.*
- *This method can effectively help to determine process bottlenecks.*

3.4. Cloud services

SCRUM is a cloud service provided through the Internet. There is no need to install a server computer to the user environment. In many cases, operators in the manufacturing industry face difficulty in using a keyboard. However, SCRUM provides a user-friendly interface that can operate through touch screens on their mobile devices.

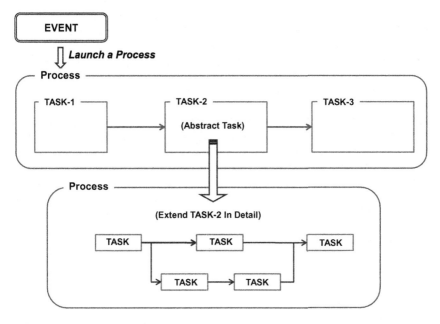

Fig. 4.   Drill-down mechanism

4. Case Study

To verify the usability of SCRUM as a business visualization tool, we applied it to Tamazawa Seiki Co., Ltd., (TAMAZAWA). Through this case study, this paper discusses how to achieve visualization in a company by using SCRUM.

4.1. About company

TAMAZAWA, located in Yonezawa city, Yamagata Pref. Japan, is a small-sized company having 14 employees. It was established in 1957 and has annual earnings of JPY 10 million. TAMAZAWA manufactures electrical terminal products using 10 Numeric Control (NC) machines. Their main product, developed for public phones, was not used as much owing to the advent of mobile phones. This led to the collapse of Lehman Brothers, and TAMAZAWA's business had been sluggish since 2010. To deal with this situation, they conducted some trials for improvement of their business. Further, TAMAZAWA's achievements show V-shaped recovery of the surplus in a year. The only thing that could not be achieved was business visualization. Under these circumstances, during the introduction of Yamagata University, I was provided with the SCRUM experimental environment in March 2014.

4.2. Background of verification experiment

TAMAZAWA custom builds various types of electrical terminal products. In the verification experiment, we used SCRUM to trace all processes from order to delivery for each product. The workflow included the following major tasks:

- *Production planning*
- *Production*
- *Quality assurance*
- *Delivery*

The goal of the experiment was to visualize the progress of these tasks.

4.3. Preparation for SCRUM verification

This section provides the details about the experimental environment configured in TAMAZAWA.

- Wireless Wi-Fi network in factory space

A network connection is indispensable for the use of SCRUM. TAMAZAWA had an office area with an Internet connection; however, Internet was not available in the factory area. Therefore, the wireless LAN network was installed in TAMAZAWA first.

- Tablet devices for each operator

Tablet devices (Android tablets) were provided to operators who were in charge of the primary production tasks. There were 10 NC machines in the factory. Some operators maintained multiple machines. The operators could access SCRUM anytime, and at any place, using their tablets. No PC or server computer was installed to use SCRUM as it was accessed from a cloud server.

4.3.1. *Release-1: initial process model*

In this experiment, we defined various process models to achieve the goal. The chart below illustrates the initial process model. The process model has a simple workflow consisting of main duties (root tasks), which include planning, manufacturing, quality assurance, and delivery connected in a series. We applied the drill down technique to the manufacturing task to observe the progress in detail.

This process and the data captured were very simple. Therefore, in the next step, TAMAZAWA requested the following:

- *Capture the machine breakdown situation.*
- *Can SCRUM start quality assurance in the middle of the manufacturing task?*

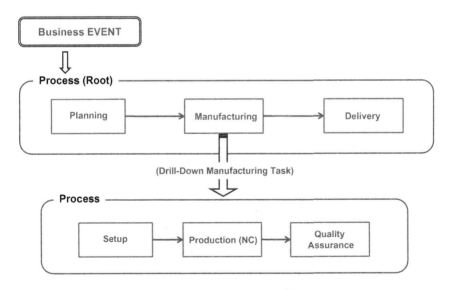

Fig. 5.   Initial process model

4.3.2. *Release-2: adding a maintenance task in NC machine operation*

Fig. 6 illustrates the expansion of the previous process model (Release-2). To include a maintenance task, an internal order was set up for each maintenance factor in the manufacturing task. Additionally, the form of the task connection in the "production process (NC)" was changed to enable the deployment of the "quality assurance task" at any time.

Next, the company requested to adapt the system to enable multiple NC machines to perform the manufacturing task for a particular order.

4.3.3. *Release-3: supporting multiple NC machine operation for an order*

Fig. 7 illustrates the expansion of the original process model (Release-3). The production process of the NC machine became independent. Additionally, the process could be called by an internal order. This

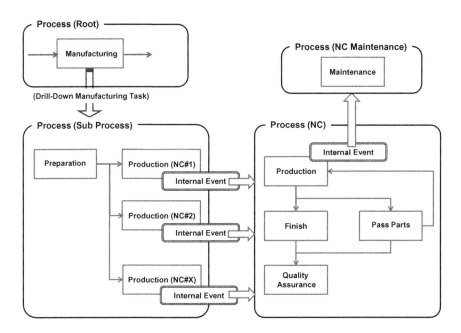

Fig. 6.   Process model — release-2

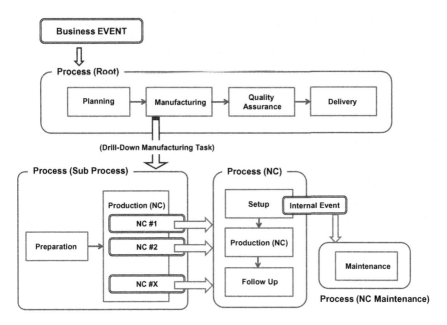

Fig. 7.   Process model — release-3

approach was similar to capturing a machine breakdown. The difference was in the state of the original task once an internal event was initiated. During a machine breakdown, the original task, i.e., the production task was paused, and then resumed following the completion of the maintenance task. However, in the case of multiple machines operating simultaneously, the state would not be changed. Moreover, the state would remain unchanged even after other machines completed production. To implement this, SCRUM maintains an attribute for each internal event registration of a task. The attribute has a task state after dispatching machine events as follows:

- DELEGATED: make "pause" a task and resume after finishing an event process.
- INDEPENDENT: launching an event. A task state is not changed (running state).

The company then requested to capture the progress of a secondary production task initiated once the primary production task was completed.

4.3.4. *Release-4: process generalization (final release)*

Fig. 8 illustrates the expansion of the process model (Release-4). Regarding the implementation of "secondary production task — follow up production" (indicated as 'follow up production' in the chart) into the process model, all production-related tasks are dispatched by internal orders. The operator may carry out any task at any time, any number of times.

This is the final form of the process. Almost all work activities that can occur in the field can now be recorded by the operator through SCRUM. Through this experiment, by using the method of extending a workflow incrementally, it has been demonstrated that a reduction in installation lead time, cost, and operator load can be achieved.

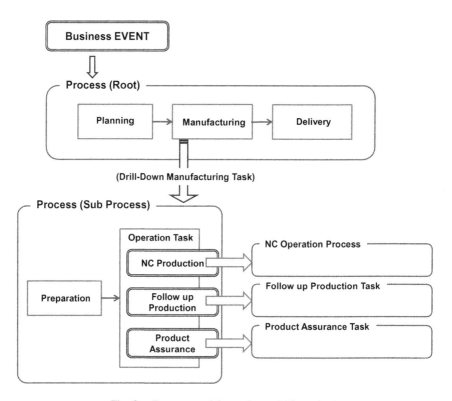

Fig. 8.   Process model — release-4 (Overview)

4.3.5. *Existing usage environment*

The application of SCRUM in TAMAZAWA took approximately 5 months, and SCRUM was used formally as a core business information system since July 2014. TAMAZAWA's staff exports the SCRUM data to the PC and analyzes the company business performance by using Microsoft® Excel®. Additionally, because SCRUM is aware of the NC machine status (Inactive/Active), a new system, "TACKLE", is employed in the workshop space. TACKLE shows the status, production volume, progress, and finish time for all machines on a large-sized TV in the workshop space for the operators to view.

5. Recent Development in SCRUM

In March 2015, SCRUM PRO, specializing in the manufacturing industry, was released. The following are the main functions of SCRUM PRO.

5.1. *Round-robin process*

The structure of an "internal order" became a frequent use of the process expression and realized communalization, however, there was a fault that a procedure to constitute it was complicated. This corrects the fault, and the process structure that allows the user to choose any task and carry it out is a "round-robin task". The round-robin process is similar to the structure of a normal process. The differences are follows:

- *Each independent task in a process does not need to have a mutual connection relation.*
- *The round-robin process must have a "terminator task" that triggers the finish of the process.*

An operator can carry out the task defined within a round-robin process at any time. Unlike an internal order, the link between an event and a process is not necessary. Similar to an internal order, it can be built easily for a flexible process structure.

5.2. *OEE extensions*

Overall Equipment Effectiveness (OEE) is a methodology to measure manufacturing productivity by evaluating equipment usage and operations. SCRUM records process execution details including the start/end time, object, operator, and tasks performed (e.g., production, break down, etc.). Using these data, SCRUM can derive the OEE scores. The OEE extension will be implemented as a new feature in SCRUM.

6. Conclusion

I would like to thank TAMAZAWA for providing us the opportunity to apply SCRUM to its business to study its effectiveness as a business visualization tool. This experiment provided the opportunity to receive feedback and improve the functionalities of SCRUM. SCRUM has been developed to provide a method of "business visualization" for SMEs. Through this experiment, I have demonstrated SCRUM feasibilities and cost effectiveness. It is a very useful tool for process measurement and/or finding the bottlenecks in a workflow. I hope that I will introduce this story as an example of a successful method of "business visualization" to other SMEs.

Index

A calculating formula, 42
action research, 160
Activity-Based Costing (ABC), 21
admin view, 168
aggregation, 169
Alliance, 17
Amoeba Management, 164
Andon, 64
A representative value or alternative
  feature, 42

balanced KPIs, 42
balanced scorecard (BSC), 10, 12,
  41, 86
branch, 169
bureaucratic system, 60
business management, 37
business performance, 37
business process, 110, 120–122, 124,
  125
Business process collaboration, 16
Business Process Management
  System (BPMS), 7, 23, 57, 77,
  130

Business Process Modeling Notation
  (BMMN), 26
Business Process Reengineering
  (BPR), 5
business re-engineering project, 39
business strategy, 62
business-to-business (B2B), 129
business visualization, 167

Capability Maturity Model Integrated
  (CMMI), 10
capacity cost rate, 24
Capital Cost Management (CCM),
  97, 101, 104–106
cell production system, 115, 116, 118,
  120, 124
Cell-style Production System, 95
child process, 154
Cloud services, 172
Collaboration, 122
commitment, 38
Commodification, 98–101
Communications Technologies (ICT)-
  based convergence business, 129

Printed in the United States
By Bookmasters